Taunton's
BUILD LIKE A PRO®
EXPERT ADVICE FROM START TO FINISH

Trim Carpentry

Taunton's

BUILD LIKE A PRO®
EXPERT ADVICE FROM START TO FINISH

Trim Carpentry

Clayton DeKorne

The Taunton Press

Text © 2008 by Clayton DeKorne

Illustrations © 2008 by The Taunton Press, Inc.

Photographs © 2008 by Andrew Kline, except: © Carolyn Bates: pp. iii, v (middle, bottom), vi (top, bottom), 1 (top, bottom middle, bottom), 4, 24, 39 (top, top middle), 40–41, 45, 49–51, 53 (left), 56 (bottom right), 57, 60, 61 (bottom), 64, 65 (top), 68 (left), 70 (top left), 75 (Design by Tom Morris Construction of Burlington, Vermont), 76–78, 81, 84, 88 (left, middle), 89, 107 (top. bottom), 111–112, 114 (top), 120 (bottom), 121 (top left, right, middle), 122, 124–125, 128, 129 (middle, bottom), 140, 141 (middle, bottom left), 142–145, 147, 149, 151–153, 156–157, 158 (top left), 159–160, 162–164, 165 (top left, middle, right), 168–170, 172, 174 (top, bottom left), 175, 177 (bottom); ©Tim Ebert: pp. 4 (middle), 10; ©The Taunton Press, Inc.: pp. 5, 12, 17 (bottom middle), 20 (top), 22 (left), 27, 29 (top left), 30 (top right), 31, 32, 39 (bottom middle), 55 (bottom), 96 (bottom right), 102 (right), 103, 108–110, 119 (bottom left), 120 (top), 127 (bottom), 165 (bottom); © Robert Perron, photographer: p. 58 (left); ©Eric Kvalsvik: p. 58 (middle); Karen Tanaka, ©The Taunton Press, Inc.: p.p 59 (top left), 82 (top left, top right), p. 126 (middle); ©Chipper Hatter: p. 59 (bottom left); ©Rob Karosis/www.robkarosis.com: pp. 59 (top right), 83 (bottom); ©Patrick Cudahy: p. 63; © Philip Clayton-Thompson: pp. 82 (bottom), 177 (top); © Ken Gutmaker: pp. 83 (top), 155 (bottom right); © Eric Kvalsvik: p. 104; Charles Miller © The Taunton Press, Inc.: p. 105 (left); © Eric Roth: p. 105 (bottom right); ©Brian Vanden Brink, photographer: p. 105 (top right), 155 (bottom left), 176 (middle); ©david-duncanlivingston.com: pp. 126 (left), 155 (top); Charles Miller and Reese Hamilton, ©The Taunton Press, Inc.: p. 127 (top); © Craig Wester: pp. 129 (top), 132 (top), 134, 159 (top right); © Jim Price: p. 131; © Louis MacKell: p. 132 (bottom); © Chris Holden: pp. 138, 141 (top, bottom right), 167, 171, 174 (right); © Grey Crawford: p. 154 (top); © John Hall: p. 154 (bottom); ©Susan Teare: p. 176 (left)

The Taunton Press
Inspiration for hands-on living®

The Taunton Press, Inc., 63 South Main Street, P.O. Box 5506, Newtown, CT 06470-5506

e-mail: tp@taunton.com

EDITORS: Andrew Wormer and Jennifer Renjilian Morris

COPY EDITOR: Betty Christiansen

INDEXER: Jay Kreider

COVER AND INTERIOR DESIGN: Kimberly Adis

LAYOUT: Cathy Cassidy

ILLUSTRATOR: Mario Ferro

Build Like a Pro® is a trademark of The Taunton Press, Inc., registered in the U.S. Patent and Trademark Office.

Library of Congress Cataloging-in-Publication Data

DeKorne, Clayton.

  Trim carpentry / Clayton DeKorne.

      p. cm. -- (Taunton's build like a pro : expert advice from start to finish)

  Includes index.

  Rev. ed. of Trim carpentry and built-ins. 2002.

  ISBN 978-1-56158-943-2

  1. Trim carpentry--Amateurs' manuals. 2. Built-in furniture--Design and construction--Amateurs' manuals. I. DeKorne, Clayton. Trim carpentry and built-ins. II. Title.

TH5695.D45 2007

694'.6--dc22

                                    2007003180

Printed in the United States of America

10 9 8 7 6 5 4 3 2 1

Construction is inherently dangerous. Using hand or power tools improperly or ignoring safety practices can lead to permanent injury or even death. Don't try to perform operations you learn about here (or elsewhere) unless you're certain they are safe for you. If something about an operation doesn't feel right, don't do it. Look for another way. We want you to enjoy the craft, so please keep safety foremost in your mind whenever you're in the shop.

For my daughters, Helen and Cecelia, who waited patiently while I was hunched over the computer, saying far too many times, "Just a minute, I'll be right there."

ACKNOWLEDGMENTS

To write this book, I am indebted to both of my fathers: Jim DeKorne, who taught me to be a good mechanic in every trade I've undertaken, including writing, and Rick McKinney, whose unconditional love for me has been a constant source of renewal. I am also deeply grateful to J. Ladd, who shared his carpentry expertise and shaped my practice in the trade.

I could never have completed this book without the loving support of Robin Michals, whose partnership over the last few years has sustained me more than words can say. I also greatly appreciate the excellent friendship of David Crosby, Christopher Pierson, John Wagner, and Pete Young, as well as the inspiration to do great work, as shown by Karel Bauer, David Dobbs, Jen Mathews, and Steph Pappas.

To complete this book, special thanks goes to Carolyn Bates and Andrew Kline, whose photographs provide far more insight into the work presented than my words ever could, and to

Andrew Wormer and Jennifer Renjilian Morris, who provided editorial guidance and supreme patience for the duration of this project.

Finally, I wish to thank the many carpenters, contractors, building suppliers, and other trade experts who shared their knowledge and never hesitated to give me their time and attention. Chief among them are Larz Allen, Tom Morse, Clark Sargent, Craig Tougas, Paul and the rest of the crew at Gregory Supply, and Dave and Bruce of Sterling Hardwoods. In addition, I owe great appreciation to a number of excellent teachers of the trades, including Sal Alfano, Charles Berliner, Butch Clark, Jed Dixon, Don Dunkley, Steve Farrell, David Frane, David Gerstel, Carl Hagstrom, Will Holladay, Mark Luzio, Craig Savage, and Dave Severance. If you ever get the chance to be on a crew with any of the characters I've mentioned on this page, count yourself extremely lucky.

CONTENTS

INTRODUCTION

Since I wrote the first edition of this book, I've heard from many readers, and their input is reflected in this new edition. We have clarified the techniques with easy-to-follow step-by-step instructions and updated information. To show you some of the many ways you might incorporate these projects into your home or your clients' homes, we've created a Design Options spread at the end of each project chapter. There you'll find different looks that go beyond the construction basics of the text and show you what else is possible. We've also added a glossary to make it easy for you to look up any terms you're not familiar with.

In this book, I have set out to provide readers with a sense of what to expect when they gather the tools and materials to undertake an interior trim job. I have poured into these pages my insights about how materials behave over time, collected design details that will look good over the long term, and disclosed many trade tips that other professional carpenters have shared with me during the past 25 years.

Carpentry books often fail, I think, when they try to cover every conceivable way to accomplish a task. The result is a mass of information that is boiled down into neat but irrelevant categories or tucked into bland generalities that wander away from the actual experience of completing a carpentry job. Instead, I have tried to avoid giving too much general information. I've focused on a few methods that have worked well for me as a professional trim carpenter.

Trim carpentry, as I address it here, refers to any kind of interior woodwork in a house, including door and window casings, baseboards, crown and ceiling moldings, wainscoting and other wooden wall paneling, cabinets, and built-in furniture. This book covers most types of "finish" woodwork—the carpentry details that are addressed before the painting and decorating begin. This book does not include specific details about the installation of doors and windows (which are better handled as part of the building envelope) or stairways (which are complex enough to fill an entire book).

Overall, this book focuses on the mechanics of how trim fits together. However, I feel strongly that no carpentry work can ever be separated from design or from building science. Carpenters must constantly make aesthetic decisions concerning proportion, scale, texture, color, and pattern, and like every other aspect of the trade, successful trim design is the result of conscious, informed effort, not accident. Equally important, carpentry is always closely tied to the physical properties of wood. Wood mechanics must always be addressed from the perspective of dimensional stability. How much a board moves dictates how tight a joint will remain.

When you understand carpentry, there are no strict boundaries among these perspectives—they are each part of a whole way of thinking that is inseparable from the actual work. Above all, carpentry requires a way of thinking about the constructed world that cannot be learned in a book. At some point, a reader must pick up the tools and actively work with the materials. At that point, I hope the principles and methods described here will make that practice a richer experience.

As you read this book, bear in mind that I have written it from the perspective of a professional carpenter, adopting a "trade" perspective that equally values production and quality. *Quality* is always a relative term. I have done jobs for customers who inspected miter joints with a magnifying glass and for others who didn't particularly care what the joinery looked like, as long as they could list "natural hardwood" in a rental advertisement. Doing each job "well" meant discerning completely different levels of quality.

The balance between production (getting the job done as efficiently and inexpensively as possible) and quality (executing it as elegantly and precisely as possible) sets a baseline for building practice. It's a baseline that works equally well for aspiring carpenters who wish to pursue the trade for its own sake and for homeowners who want the work they do to last for the next generation. That said, I feel confident that the methods described in this book will allow you to accomplish professional results.

PROJECT PLANNING

While you may be tempted to jump into a project with tools in hand, take time to plan your project first. A few key development "documents" can make the difference between success and frustration. Think of it like managing your finances. One approach is to jump in and fly by the seat of your pants, keeping the entire project in your head and tackling each task as it occurs. If you're extremely lucky, you'll complete your project without overspending your budget or taking more time than you have available. Or, you can start with a careful assessment of the project. Itemize each step, carefully estimate the costs and time, and make sketches and lists. Even a relatively simple interior trim project requires thoughtful planning. Do this before you start, and the project will begin to take shape in your mind and on paper. The reward will be efficient, smooth construction and a great finished result. ▶ ▶ ▶

Sketching a Design

Interior trim projects can range from the relatively simple to the relatively complex. Even if you just run baseboard or case a window, you'll want to consider such questions as these: How will this new work relate to the existing house? How will the horizontal planes of my window trim line up with the horizontal lines of the room? How will the vertical lines relate to each other? Does the ornamentation of these moldings fit the design period of the house? How far will this rail stand out from the wall? Will it stand out farther than the window casing, and if so, how will I finish the ends? These are the kinds of questions you need to resolve at the design phase of a project.

For me, the easiest way to work out a design is to make a series of drawings. I think best when I can see what I'm thinking about. So from the outset of any project, I take up a pencil and start sketching.

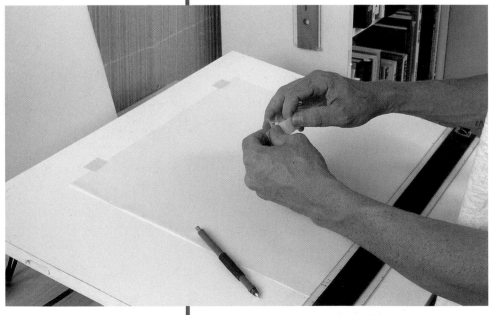

A simple drafting setup—a drawing board, a sliding square, and vellum held down with drafting tape—makes it much easier to sketch ideas and create working drawings.

For some projects, such as running baseboard, it's not necessary to go through all the drafts I define here—a simple conceptual floor plan, with dimensions for each wall, will usually be enough to give you the information you need to make a cut list and get started. However, if you're unsure about the height of the baseboard in proportion to other elements in the room, you may want to draft a detailed elevation that situates the baseboard in relation to the height of the doors, windows, and ceiling.

More complex projects call for more detail. A window stool should be carefully drawn in plan so you know exactly how wide and how long to cut the horns. You may want to draw a scaled elevation of wainscoting so that you can envision how high the chair rail will be and think through how it intersects with windows and doors. And a full wall of bookshelves or a built-in entertainment center calls for a complete series of sketches to work out everything from the massing of upper and lower units to the shelf intervals for books, electronic equipment, and even art objects. For more involved projects, I begin with a set of conceptual models, then draft a set of detailed drawings that show the project in different planes. These preliminary drawings finally evolve into dimensioned drawings from which I actually pull off construction measurements. This three-phase progression can result in one final sketch or a ream of drawings that together compose a carefully considered approach to the project.

Any sketch or detailed drawing only provides an ideal map. When you walk into the room that you will trim out, the floor and walls won't be composed of the perfect rectangles and right angles you have just drawn. And the material you use will have dimension, differing markedly from the plans and elevations you have drafted.

Align the shelf top to the head casing.

Match the sill overhang at the window.

The countertop overhang matches the overhang of the windowsill

Equal units

Equal width of window sash

Conceptual Sketch

When planning a project, begin by sketching the basic items that you intend to build. The drawing need not be elegant. At this point, you are concerned with only the general massing of components and the possible correspondence of shape to existing features, such as a window.

Annotated Sketch

After an initial sketch has defined the components, add detail by thickening the edges and working out critical alignments. Include notes that will help define the finished measurements.

Despite these limitations, however, the drawings serve an all-useful organizing purpose. I keep the drawings with me on a clipboard, along with plenty of blank paper for making notes and revisions. I start making notes to myself in the margins of the drawing and later expand those notes into material and cut lists.

Step 1: Conceptual sketches

The most important part of the design process is the early conceptual stage. Don't worry too much about drawing to scale at this point. If you don't feel very practiced, you may want to draw on vellum over th e graph paper. However, the grid on the graph paper should only be used as a rough measure for casting things proportionally. Don't get hung up on the precision of the grid. Focus more on getting a look and feel. Conceptual drawings should focus on form, not detail. They are a way of defining the basic shapes and carving out the space that the new project will occupy.

I start with a simple perspective view. Even if you're not practiced in all the rules of perspective drawing, you can sketch out simple 3-D boxes that can be developed to show the massing and shapes of your project (see the sidebar on p. 8). Don't overdo this; it should be fast. But it will help you think about how the solid form fits into the space of your home. Does a cabinet project too far out from the wall? What is the proportion between the height of the baseboard and the ceiling height of the room? How wide should the windowsill be to pick up the built-up casing? The more realistically you can see these details beforehand, the smoother the project will go.

Those who are inclined to doodle on scrap paper will be more comfortable with making conceptual drawings. For others, it will prove frustrating to draw in a loose style that doesn't look anything like what you have in mind. If this is the case, you should still make a stab at Step 2, creating preliminary plan and elevation views of the project.

TRADE SECRET

High-quality vellum won't disintegrate as you erase. Most vellum is translucent, too, so you can see a piece of graph paper beneath it or trace over a previous draft of your drawing. Use drafting tape, not masking or Scotch® tape, to secure the drawing to the drawing board.

PRO TIP

A drawing board can be as simple as plywood propped up on a 4x4 block. Make sure you keep the surface of the board smooth and clean.

The Basic Box in Perspective

SKETCHING IN 3-D PERSPECTIVE doesn't have to be an elaborate process. Many of us learned how to do this as children by drawing overlapping boxes and joining them at the corners with lines, as shown here in the Method I series.

Once you get the feel for drawing a basic box, you can sketch the front face of a box and project lines off the corners at an angle. Finish the sketch by drawing the "back" lines parallel to the top and sides.

After you're comfortable drawing a basic box without overlapping lines, you can create more complex sketches by stacking a series of boxes to represent the base and upper cabinet units, as shown.

A T-square, which slides on the edge of a drawing board, and a triangle allow you to draw right angles instantly anywhere on the page.

Try a plain HB drawing pencil for most lines and a softer B pencil for bold outlines. For erasers, try artist's kneading rubber.

Method I: Getting the Idea
Drawing volumetric cubes evolves from the trick many of us learned in grade school.

I. Start with a square.

2. Draw a second square overlapping at one corner.

3. Connect the corresponding corners.

Method 2: Learning to Sketch
The process of drawing volumetric shapes can be speeded up by sketching.

I. Start with a square.

2. Give it dimension.

3. Limit the dimensions.

4. Clean up the lines.

Stacking Boxes
When sketching interior cabinets, think in "boxes" of various sizes. These will actually be similar to the units that you will build.

Short, squat (base unit)

Narrow, tall (shelf unit)

Combined

Step 2: Preliminary drawings

The purpose of preliminary drawings is to create a series of pictures that accurately portray the finished project. Each of these pictures represents a different plane: the bird's-eye view that gives you a plan, the imaginary slice through the work that yields a section, and the flattened front view that results in an elevation.

At this preliminary stage of drawing, don't worry too much about dimensions. Instead,

Scaling Drawings

SCALE REFERS TO BOTH THE RULER and the proportions used by carpenters and architects to create measured drawings. As proportions, a scale expresses a precise relationship between a design drawn on paper and a full-size object.

Scale is expressed numerically as a proportion—for example, ¼:1, which means that every ¼ in. measured on a drawing equals 1 ft. measured in physical space. On a scale ruler, every fractional inch—¼, for example—is labeled 1, 2, 3, and so on, indicating a number of feet. Common architectural scales used for working drawings are ¼:1, ½:1, 1:1, and 3:1. In each case, the first number always implies a measurement in inches, the second always means 1 foot.

The scale you choose for measured drawings depends on the amount of detail you need to show. For most working drawings of large areas—an entire wall of cabinets or the floor plan for a baseboard layout, for example—I typically draw in ¼:1 scale (¼ in. = 1 ft.). For more detailed work, I use a 1:1 scale (1 in. = 1 ft.). For complex details, however, it often helps to magnify the drawing with a 3:1 scale (3 in. = 1 ft.).

Scale rulers come in a variety of shapes and sizes. Make sure you use an architect's scale, which is calibrated in ³⁄₃₂-in.-, ³⁄₁₆-in.-,

These three architect's scales show proportional distances divided in feet and inches (see the close-up below).

On the 1:1 scale, the first 1-in. increment is broken into 12 divisions for laying out scaled inches.

⅛-in.-, ¼-in.-, ⅜-in.-, ½-in.-, ¾-in.-, 1-in.-, 1½-in.-, and 3-in.-per-ft. increments. Don't use an engineer's square, which is divided into 10, 20, 30, 40, 50, and 60 parts of an inch.

include furniture and lines that represent the existing structure (save dimensions for the final working drawings). By including furniture, fixtures, and wall lines, you can begin to judge the size of the project in the context of the room where it will be built. Also, experiment with line weights (see the bottom photo on the facing page). For example, draw the project's outlines in a heavy dark line, and then fill in all double-line walls. These heavy lines make it easier to see the layout at a glance.

Step 3: Measured working drawings

Construction drawings (or working drawings) should be drawn to scale and include dimensions written on the paper. I use an architect's scale to help me make these drawings. Most of the time, I choose a ¼-in.:1-ft. scale, unless I need to work out close-up details.

At this point, you need to know exact measurements. If you are installing window casing,

Varying Line Weights

Upper shelves (12 in.)

Countertop overhang (1½ in.)

Wash   Dry

Upper shelves (12 in.)

Base units (24 in.)

TO HELP CLARIFY an architectural drawing, vary the line weights to distinguish the different elements. Use the darkest, boldest line for outlines, lighter lines for details (such as drawer and shelf demarcation or millwork profiles), and dashed lines for underlying parts of an assembly. In some cases, it may help to heavily mark repeating units as a way of defining the piece's mass.

Well-planned built-ins can fit around existing windows and other design elements in a room. In this case, the cabinets align vertically with the windows and horizontally with the window treatments and sill heights.

you must know the exact window dimensions. If you are building an entertainment center, you need to know the exact dimensions of the television set, estimate the number of videos you want to store, and know the size of any stereo equipment that will be included. You should also account for the exact locations of electrical switches and outlets, heating ducts, and any other house features that intersect with your project.

For any large project, dimensioned construction drawings are a must. If your trim work is part of a larger project that requires a building permit, an inspector will insist on seeing dimensioned drawings. Similarly, if you need to hire an electrician or a plumber to move wires or pipes, it's good to have clear construction drawings when discussing the estimate. It will inform the subcontractor of exactly what you want and may even save you money if the sub doesn't have to guess at unknowns and pad the price to cover them.

Material Takeoffs

Once you have a workable set of dimensioned drawings, you are ready to do a material take-off. This estimate not only serves as a shopping list but also helps you categorize the distinct tasks involved in executing the work. I begin by making notes in the margins as I develop my drawings. These notes relate not only to the inconsistencies in the actual dimensions of a room (which corners are out of square, where the floor or ceiling dips, where the drywall stands out from the window jamb, and so on) but also to the specifications for the project. This is a good place to begin keeping track of all the little decisions that go into a construction project: What is the wood choice? How wide is the casing? How thick is the window stool? What hardware will be needed?

When working up a design, you have already made a lot of decisions about the materials you need. By transferring the margin notes to a list, you have the beginnings of a material list. But that approach to generating such a list is somewhat haphazard, consisting only of those items that jump out at you as you work through the design. What's needed is a logical takeoff method that allows you to avoid wasting money by buying too much stock, or wasting time by not buying enough and having to make multiple trips to the lumberyard and hardware stores.

Trim takeoffs

As the name implies, a takeoff is taken off the drawings. For trimwork, I organize my list in two categories: standing trim and running trim.

Running trim refers to all the continuous horizontal moldings, such as baseboard, shoe molding, base cap, crown molding, and chair rail. This material is typically sold by the linear foot and often ordered in random lengths. When gen-

| Project | _TRIM FOR NEW ADDITION_ | Date |

Rm	Description	Material	Lengths	Total LF	Unit cost	Cost
BRM	_BASEBOARD_	_RANCH BASE/PINE_	_2—12'_ _2—10'_	_45_		
HALL	_"_	_"_	_1—16'_ _1—12'_	_30_		
BRM	_DOOR CASE_	_1x4/PINE SELECT_	_3—14'_ _1—12'_			
BRM	_WINDOW CASE_	_"_	_2—8'_ _2—10'_			
BRM	_WINDOW STOOL_	_5/4 x 6/PINE SEL._	_1—10'_			
BRM	_DOOR MOLD._	_½ x 1 HALF RD._	_RANDOM_	_60_		
BRM	_WINDOW MOLD._	_"_	_"_	_40_		

erating a takeoff for the amount needed, I work off the floor plan, totaling the lengths of the walls and writing down a linear-foot measurement. I typically don't subtract for openings when estimating baseboard unless there's an extra-wide door opening or a large bank of windows near the floor. And I add 10 percent to 15 percent extra onto solid-wood stock to allow for waste from defects, miscuts, and miters. For medium-density fiberboard (MDF) materials, which generally have very few defects, I add only 5 percent to 10 percent extra.

Standing trim refers to all of the window and door casings and sometimes the wainscoting materials. It's typically ordered in specific lengths and sold in lengths in multiples of 2 ft. In an entire house estimate, standing trim is often sold in packages for each door and window, and I find this makes it easy to calculate, even if I am just trimming out a few windows and doors. A package consists of the trim needed to case one side of a door or window.

For each package, I figure out how much I need, then translate it into standard-length boards. For example, one side of a standard 6-ft.,

8-in.-tall by 2-ft., 6-in.-wide door requires two 7-ft. lengths for the side casings and one 3-ft. length for the head casing (the extra inches allow room for the miters and splits or checks in the ends). To make ordering easy, I call for one 10-ft. piece and one 8-ft. piece. However, if I have several doors to do, I often specify 14-ft. material for all of the side casings (one length for one door's two side casings) and gang up all the head casings into one board, such as a 10-ft. piece for three doors (with 1 ft. of waste) or a 12-ft. piece for four doors.

Windows can be tallied in a similar manner, except you need to double up on the header (one length is actually the apron) and include a separate item for the stool (usually made with 5/4 stock instead of regular 1x stock). Overlay moldings on built-up casing is an exception. Since it is often composed of molding stock that's sold in random lengths by the linear foot, I tally the perimeter dimensions of the

PRO**TIP**

When drawing plans and making lists of materials, double-check your math for accuracy. Better to find a mistake on paper than to cut material the wrong size.

BASEBOARD PLAN

When working out a trim takeoff, pull dimensions off the plan, converting each length to standard lumber lengths.

BRM		HALL	
2—10 ft.		1—12 ft.	
2—12 ft.		1—16 ft.	
LF = 44 ft.		LF = 28 ft.	
+add = 4 ft.			
Total LF = 48 ft.			
4—12 ft.			

DOOR CASING		WINDOW CASING	
3—14 ft.		2—8 ft.	
1—12 ft.		2—10 ft.	
Total LF = 54 ft. = 60		Total LF = 36 ft. = 40	
STOOL 1—10 ft.			

windows and write down the number of linear feet needed, as with running trim.

Cabinet takeoffs

For cabinets and built-ins, I use three material categories: solid stock, sheet stock, and hardware.

Solid stock includes all of the face banding, edge banding, fascia, scribe strips, and hanging rails. I calculate these much as I do for standing trim, as the items are typically cut from standard-dimension lumber. However, many of the rails and stiles for cabinets are ripped from wider stock. For example, $1\frac{5}{8}$-in.-wide face banding and hanging rails can be cut from 1x4s (yielding two lengths per board). However, $2\frac{1}{4}$-in.-wide rail stock should come from a 1x8, which provides three lengths per board and leaves only about $\frac{5}{8}$ in. of waste (always account for a $\frac{1}{8}$-in. kerf when figuring your rips).

Sheet stock includes all of the cases, shelving, door panels, and drawer fronts. I calculate these

by the square foot, rounding up to the nearest foot. To simplify this, first calculate the square footage of a cabinet's side, bottom, and doors, and then repeat these numbers for each instance. The square footage number you obtain must be converted to a number of plywood sheets. To do this, divide the square footage by 32, the number of square feet in a standard 4x8 sheet of plywood. Here again, I round up to the next highest number to allow for some waste.

The most difficult part of a cabinet takeoff is dividing the plywood so that cabinet parts are cut from it efficiently. To clarify this process, make a drawing that shows each part you need. From that, generate a materials list, indicating a rough estimate of the square footage needed for each component and the number of sheets needed for the project. A quick sketch of a sheet of plywood will help you plan how to cut each component from that sheet. For example, this built-in (see the illustrations on the facing page) requires four sheets of $\frac{3}{4}$-in. plywood and two sheets of $\frac{1}{4}$-in. plywood to build the two lower units and the two upper units that compose it (see the top chart on p. 14).

Hardware includes all of the hinges, drawer slides, door pulls, and shelf pins, as well as any catches, bumpers, and specialty hardware, such as TV extensions or holders for CDs or DVDs. To figure this out, I mark the elevation drawings with an X at each hinge location, a circle at each pull location, and a circled X at each slide

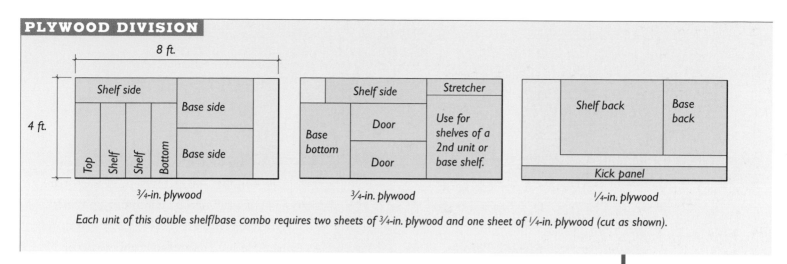

Each unit of this double shelf/base combo requires two sheets of ¾-in. plywood and one sheet of ¼-in. plywood (cut as shown).

location. To calculate shelf pins, simply count the number of shelves you plan to install and multiply by four.

With cabinets, I also include 2x4s for kick bases. I tally these by counting 2¼ ft. of 2x4 for every 1 ft. of cabinet run. This allows for a cross-piece in the ladder base approximately every 4 ft.

Supply lists

At the bottom of every list, I include a final category: supplies (see the bottom chart on p. 14). This includes all of the fasteners (nails and screws), glues and adhesives, biscuits and dowel stock, caulk, veneer tape, finishes (paints and stains), sandpaper, steel wool, wood filler, shims, extra drywall compound for repairs, and whatever else may be needed. Many of the miscellaneous items are the hardest to forecast, and they are often the things for which I go running out to a hardware store in the middle of a project. Anytime the need for one of these miscellaneous items occurs to you, write it in the margin notes of your drawing. You are most likely to think of them as you build the project in your mind and as you develop the drawings. Also, over time, you will acquire a well-stocked shop with many of these items.

Doors not shown

Pricing Materials

Once you have a complete materials takeoff, you're ready to shop at a lumberyard or home center. At most places, you can present your list at the counter and have it priced out (or, in many cases, you can fax your list if you already know the selling agent). Explain that you are getting an

Estimating Plywood for Sample Project

Base Unit = 24 in. x 30 in. x 36 in.

3/4-in. plywood	Sides	2 @ 30 in. x 24 in. = 10 sq. ft.
	Bottom	1 @ 36 in. x 24 in. = 6 sq. ft.
	Doors	2 @ 18 in. x 30 in. = 4 sq. ft.
1/4-in. plywood	Back	1 @ 30 in. x 36 in. = 8 sq. ft.

Shelf Unit = 12 in. x 40 in. x 36 in.

3/4-in. plywood	Sides	2 @ 12 in. x 40 in. = 7 sq. ft.
	Top and bottom	2 @ 12 in. x 36 in. = 6 sq. ft.
	Shelves	4 @ 12 in. x 36 in. = 12 sq. ft. (yields 2 extra shelves)
1/4-in. plywood	Back	1 @ 40 in. x 36 in. = 10 sq. ft.
		Total 3/4-in. plywood sq. ft. = 45/32 = 2
		Total 1/4-in. plywood sq. ft. = 18 = 1 sheet

Note: This is the amount of plywood needed for one base and one upper cabinet as shown in illustrations on p13.

Sample Supply List

Item	Size/type	Quantity
Shims	Cedar or pine	1 bundle
Screws	2 in. or 2½ in. (for hanging rail)	1 lb.
	1⅝ in. (for case assembly)	1 lb.
Nails	6d finish (for face frame, shelf banding, and end panels)	1 lb.
	4d ring-shank panel (for case backs)	1 lb.
	¾-in. finish brads (for door edge banding)	1 small box
Hinges	Blum self-closing #91A66304	4
Knobs	Blum mounting plate #195H7100	4
Door bumper pads	1¼ -in.-diameter maple	2
	⅜-in.-diameter clear	4
Shelf pins	Spoon, Miller #306	16 (8 extra)
Glue	Type II	1 pt.
Biscuits	#20 (for case assembly)	26 (min.)
Caulk	Phenoseal® adhesive, clear	1 tube
Wood putty		1 small can
Sandpaper	100-, 150-, 220-grit disks	1 pk. ea.
Steel wool	#0000	1 bag
Polyurethane finish	Minwax® clear, water-based	1 qt.
Brush	4-in. premium bristle	1

TRADE SECRET

Adhesives can be useful problem solvers. For example, Liquid Nails® comes in handy for holding cabinet rails where studs are missing, and a similar type of subfloor adhesive can batten down loose floorboards beneath a cabinet. My all-time favorite for securing paint-grade trim is vinyl adhesive caulk. I use it along with finish nails to affix cabinet facing, base caps, overlay moldings on casing, and chair rails.

estimate of cost figures to compare to your budget. Some places may give you a price list and let you fill in the blanks, but this is increasingly rare and not often done, unless you are a contractor buyer (in which case, you may be given password access to an online price list and purchase manager).

It's always worth comparing prices at different suppliers, but I caution you from buying solely on price. In my area, for example, I have a great hardwood dealer who offers an incredible selection, custom milling services at a reasonable price, and valuable knowledge about the woods I seek. By comparison, the largest home center offers a much better price on some of the same basic hardwoods but has a very limited selection of materials.

As you march your takeoff sheets around to different suppliers, make an effort to gather more than just a price list. See what you can learn about the supplier—strike up a friendly rapport with the agents, keep an eye out for selection, cull through the stacks, and assess the quality of the material you want for this project and others. As you learn who sells what and who offers the highest quality, the best selection, and the best service, you'll learn where to go for what items.

For example, even though I have that great hardwood dealer I mentioned earlier, I still buy all my hardwood plywood from a large home center. The home center gets its plywood from the same source as the hardwood dealer, but they order such large quantities that they can offer it at a better price. I still buy all my solid-stock hardwood from the local supplier because I get the best selection, quality, and service. While I may pay a little extra for a few solid hardwood pieces that the home center does offer, I usually end up wasting less material, because there are generally fewer defects and because I can get sizes that more closely match what I need.

Choosing Screws

In the United States, wood screws are specified by the following:

Style—Common or bugle head. On a common screw, the thread extends two-thirds the length of the screw. These days, the best option is a bugle-head wood screw, which resembles a drywall screw but has a coarser thread (see the photo at right).

Bugle-head wood screw (left), common wood screw (right).

Length—The length of a wood screw is measured from the tip of the point to the surface of the material into which the screw is driven. So the length of a flat-head wood screw is measured from the tip to the top of the head, since it is driven flat with the material, whereas the length of a round-head screw is measured from the tip to the bottom of the head, because the head remains above the material.

Gauge—Common wood screws were originally manufactured to two different standards. The overall dimensions in the two series were the same, but the number of threads differed slightly. In both series, the size is indicated by a gauge number, from #0 (approximately 1/16 in.) to #30 (approximately 7/16 in.).

From left to right: Round-head, oval-head, bugle-head, and flat-head wood screws.

Head style—Common screws come with a flat, round, or oval-shaped head. Bugle-head screws are flat with a flared (bugle-shaped) shank below the head.

Drive—Slotted, Phillips, or square (among others). I prefer using square drives, which are the least likely to slip out, or "cam out," under strain.

From left to right: Phillips-, square-, and slotted-drive screws.

MATERIALS

When you think of trim, you probably think of wood, but that's not all there is. Trim materials today include not only dimensional lumber, but also composite materials such as MDF and plastic. And panel options for built-in cabinets and shelving include much more than plywood. Today's options include composites, plastic laminates, and melamines.

Deciding which materials work best depends on how those materials will behave over the long run. The best carpenters have learned enough about these materials to become virtual wood scientists. In this chapter, you'll find some basic principles about how different woods behave in different conditions. As you sort through piles of lumber and millwork, this information will help you select the right stock for your project. You'll begin to recognize various defects and growth characteristics and understand the consequences they will have on the lasting quality of your work. ▶ ▶ ▶

PRO TIP

Don't seal the end grain of stock that will be joined with glue. Sealing prevents glue absorption and weakens the glue bond.

TRADE SECRET

After your stock has acclimated to the environment in which it will be used, make every effort to stabilize the relative humidity level in the building. Run house exhaust fans frequently. In damp climates and during rainy seasons, keep the house windows and doors closed and run a dehumidifier.

Finish Lumber

When choosing trim stock, the goal is to select straight, flat, smooth stock that will stay that way. Because wood shrinks and swells with changes in temperature and humidity, a flat, square-edged board tends to grow, shrink, cup, twist, hook, or split as it absorbs water and then dries out. Although they may seem to be fastened in place with screws, glue, and nails, miters can open and close as trim swells and shrinks, making panels warp and cabinet doors stick.

When carpenters talk about a wood's tendency to "move," they're talking about the likelihood of it changing shape, technically referred to as its dimensional stability. The dimensional stability of a piece of wood depends on characteristics inherent to that particular species and on characteristics created by sawing the wood into a specific piece of lumber. These characteristics include grain orientation, moisture content, cell structure, and the amount of heartwood versus sapwood. The presence of defects, such as knots and wane, also affects wood strength.

Wood characteristics

As trees mature, wood cells form just below the bark during the spring and summer growing seasons. These cells are hollow tubular structures. The thickness of the cell walls increases as new cells are formed during the growing season. During the winter, growth slows down and the cell wall thickness decreases. This change in cell wall thickness from one growing season to the next produces the concentric growth rings we see in a cut log. Strength and stability of any type of wood depends on the thickness of the growth layer, the thickness of individual cell walls, and the properties of the cells. These characteristics vary from species to species and also depend on the site and weather where the tree is growing.

Heartwood vs. sapwood The strength and stability of wood also depends on the age of the tree. As a tree grows, new cells (called sapwood) are added to the outer regions of the trunk and branches; meanwhile, older sapwood cells gradually change to heartwood.

The difference between sapwood and heartwood is visible in the cross section of a log (see the photo below). The outer sapwood region is lighter than the darker central heartwood. Both regions provide structural support to the living tree, but water and nutrients flow through the sapwood, as well as the inner bark. The heartwood consists of dead wood cells, and the openings that once moved water and nutrients have closed. That makes heartwood surfaces much more resistant to water movement (and shrinkage) compared to sapwood surfaces.

Moisture content The most important factor that determines a wood's stability is its moisture content (MC). Wood used for interior trim, cabinets, and flooring should be installed at an MC

The cell openings that once moved water and nutrients are closed in the denser heartwood (the darker portion of a tree). Lumber cut from this part of the tree is less prone to shrinkage and movement than the surrounding sapwood (the lighter portion).

of about 12 percent to 15 percent. Wood shrinks as it dries and swells as it absorbs water, so if you install wood with a high moisture content, the joints between two pieces will open up or the pieces will twist, cup, or split as the wood dries to match lower indoor humidity levels. Bear in mind that a piece of wood need not be noticeably wet to have a high moisture content.

Even if you buy straight lumber with an acceptable moisture content, it won't stay that way unless you take care of it. Bring the wood indoors where it will be installed and stack it with stickers—thin pieces of wood inserted between the boards that will allow air to circulate and help the wood acclimate to indoor humidity levels. If you store lumber in a damp basement or garage shop, or if the weather is especially humid, the boards will absorb water from the air and swell.

One of the most reliable ways to ensure an acceptable moisture content is to make sure you buy stock from a reputable dealer. Established lumberyards and hardwood dealers will usually stand behind the material they sell. If you are buying directly from a mill, make sure you talk to someone about the moisture content so that you don't end up with green or uncured stock. Mills usually have a moisture meter, so ask someone to verify the moisture content. It should be no higher than 20 percent; less than 15 percent is even better. (In drier regions of the country, wood often has an MC of 12 percent or less.)

Wood rarely dries evenly. This imbalance of moisture content can destroy the wood, which commonly distorts, or warps, as it dries. Because of the way wood cells operate, wood tends to warp in specific ways (see the illustration at right and the top photo on p. 20). Often it bows (warps along the length), hooks (warps along the width), or twists (warps along the width and the

Often, warping occurs as individual boards dry in the lumberyard, so it's important to examine them carefully by sighting along their edges. Your eye can be a very accurate gauge of straight lines and square corners.

Sort materials carefully and cull out the bowed, cupped, twisted, and hooked pieces.

WARPED WOOD

These are examples of warp—the distortion of a piece of wood caused by uneven shrinkage.

Twist

Bow

Cup

Diamonding

Kink

Crook

Vertical-grain material (bottom) tends to be much stronger and more stable than flat-sawn material (top).

LUMBER ORIENTATION

The grain pattern is determined by the place at which the board is sawn from the log.

A. Vertical grain
B, C. Flat grain

Elaborate figures in wood can include ray fleck (left) and bird's-eye grain (right).

depth). Cupping occurs when a board becomes uneven across the width due to unequal shrinkage between the board's two faces. Cupping is more pronounced in flat-grain than in edge-grain boards.

Lumber characteristics

Not all the wood coming from a single log is of the same quality. A lot depends on where the lumber is cut from the log. Wood changes shape least along its length (the dimension parallel to the grain) and most along its width and depth. Which dimension changes depends on the orientation of the grain.

Grain orientation The grain orientation is determined by the place at which the board is sawn from the log (see the illustration on the facing page). Because most boards are cut square from a circularly growing tree, the grain lies somewhere between a completely flat-grain board and an edge-grain (or vertical-grain) board. On most lumber, the grain is oriented somewhere between these two extremes.

Knots Knots form where branches grow off the main trunk of a tree. Knots formed by living branches are usually intergrown with the surrounding trunk, remaining an integral part of the wood. These are called tight knots. Knots from dead branches often become encased in later trunk growth and are usually found in the central

A loose round knot (far left) and a large spike knot (near left) are unstable and should be cut out of a board. Tight, round pin knots (center) are acceptable for paint-grade material.

FSC-Certified Woods

IN RECENT YEARS, the Forest Stewardship Council (FSC) has called attention to the rapid destruction of tropical rain forests where many of today's hardwoods are grown. FSC has established an international standard that has become widely accepted as the most rigorous and comprehensive in establishing a clear chain of custody to track the origin of a piece of wood to a responsibly managed forest. Today it's not uncommon to find the FSC label on a variety of trim materials in home centers.

While FSC deserves enormous credit for raising public awareness about destructive timber harvesting, there is a common misconception that FSC-labeled material is a higher-grade material. The FSC label actually has nothing to do with material quality, and it is not associated with dimensional stability, reduced defects, color consistency, or any other characteristics that we typically associate with a lumber grade.

portion of a large trunk. These knots (sometimes referred to as black knots) are often loose when the trunk is sawn; if they fall out, they become knotholes.

All knots vary in size and shape, depending on the orientation of the boards cut from the trunk. A knot split radially by the saw extends across the face of the board and is called a spike knot. Avoid boards with spike knots that extend across all or most of the face, as these boards will likely break at that point.

When the board is flat-sawn, knots appear as rounds or ovals and are called round knots. If they are smaller than ¼ in. in diameter, they are called pin knots. The form, size, and amount of knots on a given piece of lumber—and whether they are intergrown or loose—are all taken into account when lumber is graded.

Lumber grades

A single sawn log yields lumber of many different qualities. These lumber qualities are sorted, or graded, so buyers can select the type best suited to their needs. Grading is done by visually inspecting lumber at the sawmill. Softwood used for trimwork is graded for appearance only, not for strength. Graders look for the shape, size, and frequency of knots; checks (splits along the grain, mostly at the ends of boards, caused by uneven drying); pitch pockets (discrete concentrations of resin in softwoods); shake (separation of the growth rings, usually near the pith); and stain (discoloration often caused by fungi).

In other words, grading finish lumber is all about identifying appearance defects. In contrast, structural grades select for strength characteristics, such as grain deviation, density, and growth rings per inch. Therefore, softwood and hardwood finish lumber have separate grading systems.

Softwood lumber grades In general, softwoods fall into select and common grades. These grades are then divided into categories. Simply put, higher, or select, grades have fewer defects; lower, or common, grades have more.

Hardwood lumber grades Most hardwood is delivered to a millwork shop rough-sawn into general thicknesses, which are designated as 4/4 (about 1 in.), 5/4 (about 1¼ in.), 6/4 (about 1½ in.), 8/4 (about 2 in.), and so on. Typically, hardwood is sold in this rough form in random lengths and widths and usually in a green condition.

Hardwood vs. Softwood

Southern yellow pine (right) is hard and dense compared to Eastern white pine (left.) Technically, both are softwoods, however.

Grading is done when the lumber is in this rough condition. The most common hardwood-grading rules used in the United States are those established by the National Hardwood Lumber Association[SM] (NHLA). These rules specify the percentage of the total board surface (called surface measure, or SM) that can be cut out in the form of rectangular, clear-faced pieces (called cuttings). Here, *clear-faced* means free of knots, wane, shake, and checks.

The highest grade commonly sold is firsts and seconds (FAS), which yields 80 percent to 90 percent clear material. It is the most reliable option if you are looking for a uniform surface to finish naturally. However, FAS material is also pricey. I typically use it only when I need long lengths of clear material and don't have the option of cutting out or otherwise avoiding small defects.

When price is considered, the best all-around grade is No. 1 Common, which yields about 65 percent clear material. For many jobs, No. 2 and No. 3 Common work well. These lower grades have some defects but generally not as many as softwood materials of the same designation. If I buy at least 10 percent more material than I need, I usually can cut out the few knots or relegate pieces with knots and other small defects to hallways, closets, and other less visible locations.

Plywood

Plywood is always my first choice for built-ins. When quality is more of a consideration than price, I almost always choose ¾-in.-thick veneer-core plywood. For paint-grade built-ins, I opt for birch-faced plywood, which takes paint exceptionally well. For natural-finish cabinets,

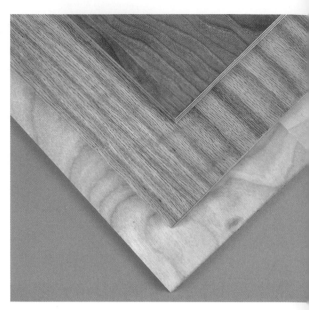

While the core of hardwood plywood is often the same, the hardwood face veneers vary for different looks. From top to bottom: cherry, oak, birch.

I usually choose maple-, oak-, or cherry-face veneer—whatever fits best.

As the name suggests, plywood is made from numerous plies of thin wood, called *veneer*. These thin sheets of wood are peeled from a tree round. Both the core (the inner layers) and the face (the outer layers) are considered veneer, though thickness and quality vary. The best wood is used for the face, while the core is made from the most plain, even slightly flawed wood. The core layers are laminated in alternating directions, so the grain of one layer runs crosswise to the other. Because of these alternating layers, plywood is much stronger and more stable than solid wood.

Panel thickness

Like most sheet goods, plywood is commonly available in thicknesses ranging from ¼ in. to 1⅛ in. I build nearly all built-in cases from ¾-in.-thick material. This thickness provides ample strength for joining the edges of pieces together

Paint Grade vs. Stain Grade

ALTHOUGH CARPENTERS constantly refer to softwoods and hardwoods, they more often make a distinction between paint-grade and stain-grade materials. The latter two categories represent types of wood and the precision level of the accompanying work. Paint-grade work relies on a painter to make it all look good. Joints can be caulked and blemishes filled. Stain-grade work, on the other hand, receives a clear finish, so the joints must be tight and the carpenter must pay close attention to the grain pattern and surface texture.

COMMON PAINT-GRADE OPTIONS

Take care even when choosing paint-grade wood. Large defects like knots show through even the most finely painted surfaces unless you spend a lot of extra time filling, sanding, and sealing them. Some good options are:

• Idaho and Eastern white pine

• Poplar

• Finger-jointed stock

• MDF board stock

COMMON STAIN-GRADE OPTIONS

Stain-grade woods focus attention on the figure in wood. Figure includes not only the grain patterns but also the textures and appearances that different wood species and different cuts can take. Here are some closed- and open-grain options to choose from:

Closed-Grain Woods

• Clear pine

• Southern yellow pine (prominent grain)

• Eastern white pine (uniform appearance)

• Vertical-grain fir

• Maple

• Birch

Open-Grain Woods

• Red and white oak

• Ash

• Mahogany

Closed-grain woods (from left to right): clear pine, maple, and birch.

Open-grain woods (from left to right): red oak, mahogany, and ash.

and tends to stay very flat. To save money or to create a lightweight, portable cabinet, ½-in. stock can be used for short shelving runs. However, this thinner material presents problems when joining pieces for built-ins. For cabinet backs and finished end panels, I typically use ¼-in. stock. For exposed cabinet backs (such as those on an island cabinet), I prefer to use ⅜-in.-thick plywood. For the backs of bookshelves and built-in cabinets, I generally use nominal ¼-in. lauan secured with wood glue and 1-in. ring-shank nails.

Lauan panels actually measure 5.5mm thick (¼ in. = 6.35mm). The panels are measured in the metric system because they are imported

SAFETY FIRST

Heavy panel stock, such as ¾-in. plywood and medium-density overlay (MDO), can be a real backbreaker. If possible, get help when moving sheets. If you must carry sheets by yourself, balance the sheet from the center, holding the bottom and top edges, as shown. In this case, the shop has been sensibly arranged, with the distance between the storage area and the tablesaw short enough so that the panels are always supported.

WHAT CAN GO WRONG

All lauan is made for exterior use, and wetting it will not affect its strength once it has dried out (though some face checking may appear). This is true of all exterior plywoods. Don't wet hardwood plywoods, however. They are made with an interior glue that isn't waterproof, so they'll delaminate.

Lauan plywood is a suitable material for cabinet backs. It's available with one side faced with hardwood veneer, which is appropriate for the inside face of cabinets.

from the Pacific Rim, where lauan (a type of fast-growing mahogany) is harvested. You can buy lauan just about anywhere, and it is the most affordable plywood option. Three face grades are available: BB, CC, and OVL (overlay). Knotholes ¾ in. in diameter are permitted in the face of the worst grade (OVL) if they are puttied. The grade is often stamped on the edge.

Lauan is available with a hardwood veneer on one or both surfaces for naturally finished cabinet backs. For exposed backs, such as those on an island shelf, I prefer to use ⅜-in.-thick hardwood plywood. The reason for this is simply strength. I once watched a fast-moving 12-year-old boy put his foot through a hardwood-faced lauan cabinet back. This was an accident, but it still proved very difficult to repair.

Plywood dimensions

Plywood is always designated first by the short-grain dimension, and then by the long-grain dimension. Mostly, you will see 4x8 material in which the grain runs along the 8-ft. dimension. Occasionally, you may find 8x4 panels. Called

counterfront plywood (and typically a special-order item), these panels have face grain running along the width of the sheet, providing evenly matched grain for cabinet fronts.

Plywood is also offered in longer lengths— 10-ft.- and 12-ft.-long sheets—as a special-order item. As you'd expect, you will pay a high premium for these nonstandard materials. But for exceptionally tall or long runs of cabinetry, these special configurations are well worth the cost.

Core options

Plywood is a two-part material, with face veneers on each side sandwiching the core. The core in most hardwood plywood is typically made from lower-grade laminations of hardwood than the face veneers. Poplar, birch, and mahogany are common woods used, either as a *lumber core* or as a *veneer core*.

Lumber-core plywood A special-order item from most lumberyards, lumber-core plywood is strong and stable, and it holds screws and other hardware as well as solid wood does. But it's pricey, averaging about twice as much as com-

Most plywood is made from individual laminations of veneer layers (top). Lumber-core plywood (bottom) is a special-order material that holds edge screws better, making it an excellent option for furniture and cabinets.

For cabinets, look for high-quality material with at least seven veneer plies (bottom). Five-ply material tends to have more voids in the core (shown on the edge of the top piece of plywood).

parable veneer-core stock. Lumber-core material should have no voids—gaps where there is no wood in the plywood core. However, some imported varieties made with lauan as the core stock have voids caused by core-piece shrinkage. If possible, steer clear of these materials.

Veneer-core plywood This is the plywood you'll usually find at a lumberyard. It, too, is strong and stable and holds screws reasonably well. However, whenever you drive screws into the edge, always predrill to avoid separating the plies.

Typical furniture- and cabinet-grade plywood has five or seven plies and sometimes more. Generally, more plies indicate better quality. Five-ply material may have some voids in the core, which can present a problem with shelf pins. If a hole for a shelf pin falls on a void, the pin is likely to sag or fall out. Higher-grade seven-ply material tends to have fewer voids and is less likely to split when you are driving fasteners into the edge.

Face options

All cabinet-grade plywoods have either rotary-cut or flat-cut face veneers (see the illustration on p. 26).

Rotary-cut veneer is peeled from a spinning log in a long, continuous sheet. This type of veneer is commonly used for softwood plywood, but it tends to be a poor choice for cabinet-grade material because of its strong, unappealing grain patterns and defects caused by trying to make the curved sheet lie flat.

Flat-cut veneer is made by running the log through a stationary knife, which slices off narrow sheets. These sheets (called "flitches") are joined side by side on the panel, making for a more expensive, but also a more desirable, cabinet-grade panel stock.

The individual flitches on the face of plywood typically vary in size from sheet to sheet, and the width and number of flitches used in each sheet affect the appearance. For naturally finished cabinets, it's often worth paying close attention to how these veneers are joined together. For

Shoot Board for Cutting Plywood

A "SHOOT BOARD" first serves as a straightedge to guide the saw. But just as important, it also holds down the grain along the cut so that the blade doesn't tear out when cutting cross-grain veneer. I made my shoot board with two strips of ¾-in.-thick material, using one piece for the fence and one piece for the table. The table is the width of the shoe on my saw, which rides on the table. I use a pair of spring clamps to secure the outside edge of the board's table to the cutline on the plywood. With veneer that splinters easily, such as oak, I first score the cut along the edge of the board. I replace the table on the shoot board occasionally because different blade thicknesses chew up the edge near the blade.

ROTARY-CUT VENEER VS. FLAT-CUT VENEER

Rotary-cut veneer is cut with the log spinning into the knife to create one continuous peel. Flat-cut veneer is cut with the log moving straight across the knife to produce many narrow sheets called "flitches."

Rotary Cut

Veneer

Knifes

Flat Cut

Knife

Veneer

Softwood plywood is nearly always made from rotary-cut veneer, which allows the face to be one continuous piece. However, stresses in the peeled veneer often crack.

example, when I lay out a series of cabinet doors, I locate the seam of the book-match and measure from it in equal directions. The seam can be placed either in the center or in between doors, depending on how many different cabinet doors need to match. I also try to choose upper and lower cabinet doors from the same vertical sheet, so that the grain runs continuously from top to bottom.

Long runs of cabinetry may be built from several sheets of plywood. You can buy up to 12 sheets of flitch-matched plywood to make the run consistent. Such sheets are marked consecutively as $^1/_{12}$, $^2/_{12}$, $^3/_{12}$, and so on. However, they require placing a special order with a hardwood dealer—a luxury I don't always have. Usually, I lean full sheets of plywood against the wall and rearrange them until I obtain the most pleasing composition possible. Be sure to number the doors and keep track of each piece as you work.

Whenever possible, I use true book-matched veneers (see the top photo on p. 28). Often, slip-matched material looks convincingly like

Plywood Face Veneers

BOOK-MATCHED VENEER

To create book-matched veneer, a plywood manufacturer turns over the top flitch from a stack of consecutively sliced flitches like the page of a book, then joins these two pieces side by side. This way, the grain on one surface mirrors the grain of the next. Such pairs of flitches make up the face of a sheet of plywood.

SLIP-MATCHED VENEER

This veneer is made by joining consecutive flitches without turning them over; in this case, the grain pattern runs parallel rather than as a mirror image. This grain pattern repetition works best with especially wild and distinctive grain. However, slip-matched veneer makes it difficult to achieve a sense of symmetry in the grain design across a cabinet face. For that reason, I prefer using book-matched material, which is, fortunately, the more common of the two.

similar grain, but the wood absorbs finish quite differently, creating a distinct—and rarely accept-able—striped effect once the panels are finished (see the bottom photo on p. 28).

Plywood grades Typically, the grade of plywood is specified by the quality of the face veneers. The two faces are not necessarily of the same type or quality of veneer, so a single sheet may have two different grade face veneers. An A face—the best quality available—has no knots, splits, or other defects. B and C faces are of lesser quality but are often highly acceptable

Storing Plywood

THE BEST WAY TO STORE sheet goods so that they don't twist or bow is to keep them perfectly vertical on edge or absolutely flat and continuously supported. Full sheets of panel stock take up a lot of room, so it's often easier to store them on edge. Place them on short 2x4 blocks to keep the edges away from moisture, and keep the panels as vertical as possible. If they are stored at an angle, the weight of the panels can cause them to bow.

A good solution is to store panels as close to vertical as possible to prevent them from sagging.

True book-matched veneer has an interesting matching grain pattern, and the matching flitches absorb stain and clear finish evenly.

Slip-matched flitches often absorb finish differently, creating an unsightly striped effect.

SAFETY FIRST

When cut, the tiny fibers of MDF pulverize into a superfine dust that defies dust-collection systems. The formaldehyde-based adhesive used to bind the fibers is also irritating and possibly carcinogenic. You must wear a dust mask when cutting this material; plan to spend a lot of time vacuuming the dust as well.

WHAT CAN GO WRONG

While AC-grade fir plywood—where one face is A-grade and the other is C-grade—often looks smooth and even, it doesn't make a very good paint substrate. The grain is often raised by paint, and the face usually absorbs paint unevenly. The raised grain and patches in the face veneer usually telegraph through any finish. Look closely at the core—it often has fairly large voids. These make the edges unstable for joining and may telegraph through paint.

for painted built-ins, though if you are working with AC plywood, for example, plan on putting a C face inside the cabinet. Plywood designated AA has two A-grade faces. This is the best quality available, but it's usually a special-order item.

Composite Panel Stock

While I think hardwood plywood is the easiest and most reliable material to use for built-ins, it's certainly not the most affordable or necessarily the best. In the past decade, MDF has improved tremendously, and perhaps more than any other product, it offers the best value. Cabinet-grade particleboard has also improved and is very affordable, though I think it is the least desirable material available for built-ins.

Both MDF and particleboard are used as the substrate for panels with high-tech finishes, such as melamine and plastic laminates. These products offer outstanding performance and come in an enormous range of colors and styles, making them the products of choice for some of the finest prefabricated cabinetry on the market.

MDF

MDF is made from very fine wood fibers that are mixed with a urea-formaldehyde–based adhesive, then compressed under heat and pressure. The result is a stable material with a super-smooth surface that takes paint exceptionally well. It also makes a good substrate for plastic laminate and veneer.

MDF usually comes in sheets measuring 49 in. by 97 in., which provides plenty of area for ripping full 12-in.- or 24-in.-wide pieces. Currently, a plain, ¾-in.-thick sheet sells for about a third of the price of hardwood plywood.

Although I prefer using plywood, MDF is so much more affordable that I now use it more

From top to bottom: plywood with an MDF core, plywood with a traditional veneer core, particleboard, and plywood with a combined MDF/veneer core.

Medium-density fiberboard (MDF) is a composite material made from fine wood fibers (bottom); medium-density overlay (MDO) is a plywood product with a paper face overlay (top).

The unsealed edges of MDF absorb paint and moisture and are generally unstable. Here, you can see what the edges look like painted.

than almost any other material for paint-grade built-ins, particularly bookcases. However, it has some definite drawbacks that you must be aware of before using it. The most obvious one is weight. A full sheet of ¾-in.-thick MDF weighs close to 100 lb. (compare that to a sheet of hardwood plywood, which weighs about 70 lb.), so you definitely need help handling full sheets. Although the homogenous thickness looks uniform, the edges drink paint, so they must be banded. And just as the edges drink paint, they also absorb moisture, making the edges swell and, in extreme cases, crumble. I do not recommend using MDF in bathrooms or in any location where it may get wet.

MDF is available in a wide variety of hardwood-face veneers (for example, Georgia-Pacific® Fiber-Ply). Although this material resembles plywood, it is much more delicate. Because the surface of the MDF substrate is so smooth, manufacturers are able to use an ultra-thin face veneer that is much easier to accidentally sand through, and the edges are still quite fragile.

MDO

Not to be confused with MDF, medium-density overlay (MDO) is an exterior-grade plywood covered by a resin-treated paper. This material has a glass-smooth surface especially made for paint (see the top left photo on p. 30). It is a popular product for signs and makes a great material for built-ins, combining the advantages of veneer-core hardwood plywood with the best paint surface available. However, MDO is expensive, typically costing about 10 percent more than

WHAT CAN GO WRONG

MDF cuts cleanly with no tearout. But the corners become very fragile and can easily chip or dent when handling cutout panel pieces. Plan to use biscuits, glue, and nails for joining MDF. Screws hold poorly in the face and especially badly in the edges.

PRO TIP

MDF absorbs moisture and can crumble. Avoid using it in damp locations, such as bathrooms.

Beefing Up Particle-Board

ALTHOUGH PARTICLE-BOARD may seem like an economical choice for shelving, it's one of the flimsiest materials available. However, you can increase its strength in a number of ways:

• Gluing a ⅛-in.-thick edge band to a ¾-in.-thick particleboard shelf increases the shelf's load-bearing capacity by about 15 percent.

• Adding ⁵⁄₁₀₀-in.-thick plastic laminate to one edge and both faces increases a particleboard shelf's load-bearing capacity by about 200 percent.

• Gluing a 1x2 solid-wood apron to the front edge increases its load-bearing capacity by 300 percent to 400 percent.

These strategies will work for any material, allowing you to increase the shelf length without creating a sag.

comparable hardwood plywood. Nevertheless, you should seriously consider it for built-ins in damp locations because it is made of an exterior-grade plywood that won't delaminate when periodically exposed to water.

Particleboard

Particleboard has been around for a long time, and modern versions are vastly superior to those made 20 or more years ago. For starters, the chip size, and therefore the panel density, varies across the thickness. Larger chips fall to the core, and finer chips fall on each surface. This makes for a stable product with a smooth surface for wood veneer or plastic laminate. Particleboard is a common substrate for melamine and plastic-laminate panels. It also comes preveneered in a variety of hardwoods, mostly birch and oak.

Despite recent improvements, I am not a big fan of particleboard. Although it takes paint well, paint may raise the particles slightly, so painted particleboard is not as smooth as painted MDF. Also, particleboard is just as heavy as MDF, and the corners are just as (if not more) fragile. But because the particles are so much bigger than those in MDF, when particleboard chips or has a nail blowout, the results are much more disastrous.

Because the flakes in particleboard are so much bigger than the fine fibers in MDF, when particleboard chips or has a nail blowout, the results are much more disastrous.

And though the faces of a panel have a better screw-holding capacity, the edges do not. I generally steer clear of particleboard except when I'm using melamine and plastic laminate.

Specialty surfaces

Both particleboard and MDF are available with special finishes made of resin-saturated industrial papers. The most common and versatile ones for built-ins are melamine and plastic laminates.

Melamine Although it is often referred to as a separate panel material, melamine is a clear resin used to create a panel surface. True melamine panels use industrial paper with a basis weight of 80 grams to 140 grams. The paper comes in a range of colors and decorative surfaces (ones that mimic wood grain are the most common). The paper is thoroughly saturated with resin, laid over the substrate (particleboard, MDF, or plywood), and fed into a press, which applies heat and pressure at about 350 psi (pounds per square inch). During this process, the

Nail Blowouts

JOINING THIN PANEL STOCK presents a number of difficulties. The most common is nail blowouts. Unless a nail is centered within the edge of the panel and driven perfectly straight, it can easily blow out the sides. This happens most frequently when you use a pneumatic nailer, but it also occurs when you use a hammer or even drive screws.

To fix a blowout, use end nippers to clip off the nail below the surface. If you can't clip the nail below the surface, use a nail set to drive the cut end into the panel. Use a sharp chisel to pare down the bulged material around the blowout. Last, fill the hole with epoxy wood filler. Here, too, I use a sharp chisel to apply the filler and leave a clean surface that requires minimal sanding.

resin penetrates the substrate fibers, permanently fusing the surface to the substrate. The result is a surface that's thinner than but similar to plastic laminate.

The biggest advantage of melamine panels is that they are prefinished, and the finish is smoother and more consistent than just about any hand-applied paint. The surface is tough, wears well, and resists water. Melamine is also available predrilled and preripped for shelf stock, which offers a huge labor-saving advantage.

The downside of melamine is that it requires more elaborate joinery and the utmost precision. Glue doesn't stick to melamine, so the joints must be rabbeted (see the photo at right). And the brittle surface chips easily, requiring extra care and exceptionally sharp tools. The edges are usually taped with an iron-on polyester ribbon.

Plastic laminates Plastic laminates are made from multiple layers of paper saturated with phenolic resin, resulting in a much more rugged surface than melamine. Typically, plastic laminate used for cabinet faces and countertops has three parts: a core of layered paper saturated with phenolic resin and bonded under high pressure (about 1,400 psi), a colored or patterned

Melamine-faced particleboard provides a prefinished panel material. But the corners chip easily, so it requires ultra-sharp tools and the utmost care.

Glue doesn't stick to melamine, so the edges must be rabbeted.

Plastic laminate is a versatile material that can be used in a number of applications. Here, a post-formed countertop—a particleboard underlayment topped with a plastic laminate surface—is being prepared for a kitchen installation.

WHAT CAN GO WRONG

Nothing will make your heart sink as fast as a broken corner or a nail blowout in a pristine melamine surface. However, such an unsightly scar can be repaired using epoxy with a universal color mix. Both ingredients can be purchased from a paint store or a large hardware outlet that sells paint. Blend the epoxy and the color, and then apply the mixture with a sharp chisel. After it cures, pare it smooth. What you can't do is sand and paint this material. No matter how much you try, you will never be able to match the texture of the melamine surface.

LAYERS IN PLASTIC LAMINATE

Clear melamine top coating

Colored or patterned paper

Core of layered paper

Plastic laminate used for cabinet faces and countertops typically has three parts: 1) a core of layered paper saturated with phenolic resin; 2) a colored or patterned paper; and 3) a clear melamine top coating.

Available in a variety of trim profiles, MDF is an exceptionally stable material with a super-smooth surface that takes paint well, but freshly cut edges tend to be extremely fragile and chip easily.

paper, and a clear melamine top coating (see the illustration on the facing page). This process produces a $\frac{1}{16}$ in.-thick sheet of plastic that comes in lengths of up to 12 ft. Plastic laminate can be purchased separately from the substrate. (For more on applying plastic laminate, see "Trade Secret" at right.)

Sometimes referred to as high-pressure laminate or HPL, plastic laminate comes in an astounding variety of colors and patterns. Between the two major manufacturers—Formica® and Wilsonart®—you can match just about any color and style you could want, including faux wood, stone, leather, and fabric. Standard stock always has a dark-colored resin core that shows a brown line along the edge. However, both manufacturers also offer laminates that are the same color all the way though, making the seams less conspicuous.

Millwork

As the name implies, millwork is any lumber milled into specific profiles for different uses. This can include molding pieces with a variety of curves, such as those found on most base caps, coves, and crowns. Or it can be simple square-edged, thin pieces intended for such uses as lattice and door stop. Larger pieces, such as profiled casing and one-piece base stock, also fall into the millwork category. These days, many profiled trim pieces are made from composite wood materials, such as MDF, or from pure synthetic materials, such as urethane foam and PVC.

Lumberyard choices

Most lumberyards and home centers carry a selection of millwork, but that selection can be disappointing at times. Generally, a lumberyard buys from one millwork source, and then maybe

TRADE SECRET

Plastic laminate comes in two basic grades: horizontal and post forming. Horizontal grade, which is about $\frac{1}{16}$ in. thick, is what you should buy to apply to a substrate. Post-forming material is much thinner and is used for wrapping over the rounded edges and molded backsplash of a post-formed countertop.

Most standard trim

stock (such as casing and one-piece base-board) comes with a hollow cut on the back. This practice is called "backing out." Its primary purpose is to weaken the stock, making it less likely to cup when nailed securely in place. The hollow also allows the trim to span lumps in the wall while remaining tight at the edges.

If you're using trim that is backed out or has kerfs cut in the back, keep in mind that exposed ends will reveal the hollow (or the kerf). This means that aprons below windows must have miter returns, and butt-joined casing may need a back band.

Stabilizing Wood

WHEN MAKING YOUR OWN TRIM STOCK, it's good practice to kerf the back of wide finish lumber. The kerf achieves the same thing as the backing out on milled trim—it helps prevent the board from cupping. I typically run extra-high baseboard (made from 1x8 and greater) through the tablesaw to cut at least three ¼-in.-deep kerf lines in the back. Better still is to run the stock through a dado blade to hollow out the back.

carries only the most popular profiles from that supplier. As a result, you may be faced with only one choice of profile in each category. But it's worth doing some investigating to discover the various profile choices that may be available. Different yards may carry different profiles, and oftentimes millwork suppliers make available brochures and catalogs of their products. Ask for them, because chances are good that you can find or order a particular profile that you want to use. The trick is identifying which one that is.

Toward that education, you will have to dig around—sometimes deeply. Look in old wood-working and joinery texts. Almost any edition of *Architectural Graphic Standards* will have interest-ing examples. All of these sources will seed your imagination and interest, develop your eye for trim details, and make you more aware of wood-work details in the buildings around you.

BASIC MOLDING SHAPES

Molded trim is a combination of various basic shapes.

Ogee

Reverse ogee

Bead

Bead

Thumbnail bead

Quirk bead

Astragal

Ovolo

Cove

Dentil

Ceiling

Bed

Crown

Cove

Base

Contemporary one-piece

Colonial one-piece

Base

Cap

Shoe mold

Detail

Picture rail

Scotia

Lattice

Brick mold

Quarter round

Door stop

Screen

Half round

Window

Clamshell

Back band

Corner

Colonial

Window stool

Each period architectural style has distinct trim details. Here are examples of built-up crown, chair rail, and baseboard profiles representing three common periods.

Simplified Colonial

Reverse ogee

Cornice

Ogee base

Quirk ogee with astragal

Casing

Architrave

Quirk

Chair rail

Wainscoting

Nosing

Cove

Base

Federal

Reverse ogee crown

Cornice

Cove   Dentil

Double ovolo

Casing

Architrave

Quirk

Astragal

Ovolo

Chair rail   Cove   Dentil

Wainscoting

Cove

Nosing

Base

Greek Revival

Reverse ogee crown

5/4 fascia

Cornice

Ovolo   Cove

Double Greek ogee

Casing

Architrave

Quirk

Bead

Ogee

Chair rail   Bead   Quirk

Wainscoting

Greek ogee

Base

PRO**TIP**

If you're trying to match old trimwork, you'll probably need the services of a custom mill shop. Ask your hardwood dealer for recommendations.

Custom-cut baseboard (left) has deeper, more ornate profile cuttings than typical stock baseboard (right).

Most mill shops have a huge selection of knives that they have cut for previous jobs. The shop will still charge the fixed set-up price for bolting the knives into the cutterhead and adjusting the milling machine for your run, but this is much less expensive than cutting new knives, so be sure to look carefully at the existing profiles. A skillful operator can often make a close match with existing knives by setting up the machine to cut only a portion of the profile.

Millwork choices

Although they are expensive, custom moldings are usually your best choice for ornate trim; if you are trying to match a specific period detail, they may be your only choice. For these, you'll need the help of a millwork shop.

The milling machines in a well-equipped millwork shop have one or more cutterheads. A series of "knives" are custom-cut from steel blanks to the exact dimensions of the molding profile you need; these knives are bolted into the cutterheads. The millwork shop will charge a fixed fee for cutting the knives, so the more trim you order in a particular custom profile, the cheaper it will be per foot. Typically, the cost of a knife is figured by the inch; a set-up charge is usually added on as well. The final cost of the trim also includes a price for the wood.

Millwork that is produced on multiple-head machines costs more, since several knives must be cut for each profile. However, these machines produce a much smoother piece of trim, and the savings in sanding and finishing is usually well worth the extra cost. To order the knives, the millwork shop requires a full-scale drawing of the profile. If you are matching an existing piece of molding, bring a sample, if possible.

TRIMMING WINDOWS

Modern windows are factory-made and come preassembled as a unit that is installed in one piece into the rough opening. Many windows come with a narrow exterior trim, called brick molding, which is prefixed to the frame. And occasionally, a window unit will even include an interior "trim kit." But usually, it's up to the finish carpenter to make and install the interior trim. That's what this chapter is all about.

Of all the trimwork inside a house, window trim is among the most common and conspicuous. Because windows are usually positioned at eye level—in clear sight—the trim you install around the window will be noticed. Just because it is conspicuous doesn't mean it has to be elaborate. Good proportions, capable craftsmanship, and clean detailing can create a simple elegance that will be admired. ▶ ▶ ▶

Trim Styles

Trimming a window starts after the window unit has been installed and the walls have been insulated and covered with drywall. The interior trim covers the gap between the ragged edge of the drywall and the window frame, preferably in a style that matches the woodwork in the rest of the house.

The simplest casing method is to picture-frame the window by simply wrapping all four edges of the window with casing and mitering the casing at the corners. This style visually works best for smaller, horizontal windows and for simple trim profiles that are painted to blend with the wall. The other option is commonly called traditional window trim. This includes casing on the sides and across the top, or head, of the window, while the bottom of the window gets a stool with an apron below.

The stool often sits higher than the sill to keep wind and water from seeping in below the bottom edge of the window sash. Stock stool profiles have an angled dado that fits into the angled inside edge of the sill. If you are making your own stool, it's wise to mimic this profile to create a weatherproof seal at this critical junction. However, this isn't required with many modern window units, which have a flat inside face to which the stool simply butts.

Keep these points in mind when choosing a window trim style:

- How much attention do you want to draw to the trim?

- What kind of window treatments will you use? Wide window stools can sometimes interfere with curtains.

- How square is the window? Picture framing is much more difficult to do when a window unit is wildly out of square.

- How flat is the plane between window and wall? If the window is not exactly parallel to the walls, consider using a reveal joint, bead joint, or corner blocks to mask the discrepancy.

- How much time do you have and how complex a task do you want to take on?

Traditional trim includes casing on the top, or head, of the window (above) and a stool with an apron (right).

Anatomy of a window

Before we talk about how to trim a window, it helps to have an understanding of some basic window terminology (see the illustration at right).

Jamb extensions The frame, or jamb, of the window unit may or may not be the same thickness as the wall, and it's not uncommon for the window unit to be narrower. Andersen® window units, for example, always require jamb extensions, because the frames are only $2\frac{7}{8}$ in. thick. However, Andersen also provides extensions with a tongue that fits easily and tightly into a groove in the frame to fit standard $4\frac{1}{2}$-in. and $6\frac{1}{2}$-in. walls. Other window companies provide premade jamb extensions, too, so be sure to ask your window dealer about those options when you order your windows. While you may have to pay a little more, I've found that these factory-milled extensions are usually well worth the additional cost. However, if the windows are already ordered, the extensions have been lost, or you are refitting an existing window, you will have to make the jamb extensions yourself.

Casing These are the pieces most commonly referred to as "window trim." The casing is nailed perpendicular to the edges of the jambs and is the most conspicuous—and often the most ornate—component of window trim. Window casing covers the gap between the window and the wall and stiffens and supports the jambs.

Stool While we commonly talk about setting something down on the windowsill, carpenters often refer to this interior piece as the stool to distinguish it from the angled exterior sill. While the sill extends outdoors, past the siding, to shed water away from the building, the stool, in contrast, is flat and its front edge projects beyond the plane of the interior casing. This edge is often

ANATOMY OF A WINDOW

Header

Head jamb

Sill

Stool

Header

Head casing

Head jamb

Side jamb

Side casing

Stool

Apron

The ends of the stool (left) are cut in around the side jambs, creating a flat surface for the side casings to sit on.

PRO**TIP**

If you need jamb extensions for your windows, buy them factory milled when you order your windows. It's a tremendous timesaver.

shaped with a roundover or ogee profile, though a square-edged stool is also common. The ends of the stool typically get cut in around the side jambs, creating horns for the side casings to sit on (see the photo above). Picture-frame windows don't require a stool; instead, they simply have

When trim turns a corner, such as where a window casing meets a jamb extension, it is usually joined with a reveal. That is, the edges of each piece do not line up but instead are offset about ¼ in. This creates a step, adding an extra shadow line that contributes to the visual complexity of the trim. But a reveal also serves a practical purpose, fooling the eye and hiding any slight misalignments between the meeting pieces. Your eye can easily see when two corners don't meet, but it is less likely to notice a slight difference in the width of a reveal line.

WINDOW STOOL OPTIONS

Traditional Stool (option A)
The stool extends to the sash.

Traditional wood sash

Wood sill

Apron

Wall

Traditional Stool (option B)
The stool extends to the jamb.

Modern sash

Modern sill

Wall

Apron

Shim to support

Picture-Frame Jamb Extension
The jamb extension is the same as the head and side jambs.

Modern sash

Modern sill

Casing

Wall

a bottom jamb extension. Traditionally trimmed windows, however, always have this flat, horizontal piece, which provides a visual foundation for the casing (see the illustration at left).

Apron The apron sits below the stool. It provides support for the stool and covers the gap between the drywall and the window. If a profiled casing is used for the apron, a return is usually cut on each end.

Three standard window designs

There are a wide variety of woodwork design styles from which to choose. However, the majority of my work has always called on variations of just three basic styles.

Contemporary On nearly all of the windows that call for a simple picture frame, I apply a standard contemporary, or clamshell, casing (see the left illustration on the facing page). This material has a thinner inside edge, so it "rolls" easily to conform to window jambs that protrude or sink slightly beyond the wall plane. Basic clamshell trim is widely available in inexpensive Philippine mahogany or white pine. I prefer the pine, since most of the time I want to paint the material so it blends inconspicuously with the wall surfaces.

A contemporary design scheme calls for clean lines and minimal woodwork. If baseboard is used, it may be a simple one-piece wood or rubber cove. Ceiling trim is rarely included.

Classical I use this term loosely to refer to general designs that can be replicated using stock moldings, not as a precise design term to refer to historical restorations. A cornice molding that wraps around the head casing usually tops classical window and door trim. A reveal joint or bead joint works well to emphasize the look of a "capital." Of course, this style calls for a traditional stool and apron. I typically install an apron made from stock profiled millwork (often

CONTEMPORARY DESIGN SCHEME

Clamshell casing

One-piece baseboard

CLASSICAL DESIGN SCHEME

Crown

Cornice

5/4 head casing

Mitered return

Roundover stool

Apron

Base cap

Baseboard

Shoe mold

VICTORIAN DESIGN SCHEME

Crown

Baseboard used as frieze board

Corner block

Pilaster casing

Stool with ogee

Apron

Base cap

Molded baseboard

called Colonial casing), with the ends mitered to a return.

The classical style blends well into a room scheme that includes tall (1x6 or greater) two-piece baseboards, rectangular plinth blocks at the base of door casings, and crown moldings at the ceiling.

Victorian Trim of this period tends to be much more ornate and fanciful than trim in the more restrained classical style. Plinth blocks and corner blocks with rosettes fit well around windows and doors. Corner blocks are most often used with pilaster casings, which are milled in a symmetrical, linear design. The stool typically has a generous ogee cut along the front edge. The apron is wide, often built up with an ornate band and coped or mitered back at the ends.

The high level of ornament carries over into the rest of the woodwork as well. Elaborate crown moldings (often with an added frieze), picture rails, and chair rails with beaded wainscoting are all signature details of the Victorian period.

Jamb Extensions

The type of jamb extension you need depends on the width of the window and the width of the wall. The simplest type is a piece of square-cut stock that butts against a square window edge. I make this type if I need an extension that is less than 1¼ in. wide. It allows me to nail 8d finish nails through the edge of the piece into the window frame. In this case, I usually leave a reveal (if there's room in the rough opening), offsetting the extension from the existing window jamb.

WHAT CAN GO WRONG

A trim carpenter's worst nightmare is a window that was shimmed too tightly when it was installed. This squeezes the jambs on the window unit, causing the sash or casement to bind. Always check the operation of a window before installing the interior trim; otherwise, you will lock the problem into the wall.

Traditional Head Styles

TRADITIONAL TRIM lends itself to many variations in design, not only of the molding profile, but also in the way the head joins the sides. These details provide an alternative to simply mitering the corners and serve a practical as well as an aesthetic function. Miter joints—particularly in wider boards—are prone to opening up as the wood dries. The joints below are less apt to open up.

- Finish wall
- Head casing
- Head jamb
- Side jamb
- Side casing

The head casing and side casing often sit at slightly different planes from one another.

BUTT JOINT

The simplest method of joining the head to the side casings is with a simple butt joint. This style can be cut easily, but any misalignment between the head and the side casings will be noticeable. Also, simple butt joints only work on flat, nonprofiled casing stock. If you choose a profiled casing, you must cut a miter or use some other method to join the corners.

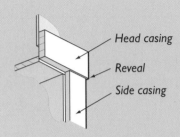

- Head casing
- Reveal
- Side casing

The head casing projects beyond the face and edge of the side casing to create a reveal.

REVEAL JOINT

If the walls aren't particularly flat or the window isn't exactly parallel to the wall, consider installing a head casing cut from thicker stock (such as 5/4), a detail commonly found in Craftsman-style homes built in the early 1900s. It creates a reveal where the head and sides join, allowing the casing to be slightly misaligned without drawing much attention.

- Head casing
- Side casing

The block projects beyond both the head casing and the side casing to create a reveal.

CORNER BLOCKS

Thicker (typically 5/4) corner blocks inserted between the head and the side casings provide an elegant detail that is common in Victorian buildings. Frequently, these corner blocks have an ornate rosette cut into the center of the square. The rosettes are cut on a drill press with an elaborate bit, or they can be ordered through specialty millwork companies.

- Head casing
- Projects same distance as stool horns
- Side casing

The bead projects beyond the face and edge of the casings to create a reveal.

BEAD JOINT

Adding a thin molding to the bottom of the head casing creates a bead joint. The molding only needs to be $3/8$ in. to $1/2$ in. thicker than the casing stock, with a very simple profile—usually a roundover.

- $1\,3/4$ ogee stop
- Head casing
- Bead molding
- Projects same distance as stool horns

The bead and ogee stop projects beyond the face and edge of the casings.

CAPITAL

For a more elaborate style, add another piece of trim along the top edge of the head casing. Combined with a bead joint, this creates a "capital."

- Back band (mitered at the corner)
- Head casing
- Side casing

The side casing butts to the head casing.

BACK BAND

Used with butt-joined or mitered casing to add an extra dimension of visual complexity to the trim, the back band also covers the end grain of butt-joined head casing. It is one of the simplest built-up casing styles.

COMMON JAMB EXTENSION PROFILES

Square Edge
This is the standard site-installed jamb extension.

Exterior sill

Window unit

Jamb extension

Wall framing

Back Stepped
This wide jamb extension (supplied by Eagle® Windows & Doors) can be made on site.

Exterior sill

Window unit

Jamb extension

Wall framing

Tongue and Groove
This manufacturer-supplied jamb extension is typical of Andersen windows.

Exterior sill

Window unit

Jamb extension

Wall framing

If the extensions are much wider, however, I need another way to attach them. In that case, I usually rip a "step" in the back face. This allows me to secure the extension with a screw through the step, or shoulder. I always preassemble these wider extensions into an extension "unit," which makes for tighter joints and a faster job.

Window prep

Before trimming any window, first check to see how well the window operates. If the window has been shimmed too tightly, this is your last chance to correct it easily. It's also your last chance to seal it well against air leaks.

1. Begin by cleaning off any drywall compound that may have collected at the edges near the rough openings.

2. Cut back any shims that extend past the window frame **A**. Not all windows need jamb extensions. Ideally, the jambs should extend about 1/16 in. beyond the wall surface. Check this by holding a square or straightedge against the wall and sliding it over the window **B**.

A

B

3. In some cases, the existing window jambs may even stand a bit proud, projecting into the room slightly. If this is the case, you may need to plane the window jambs. If the jambs project into the room more than 1/4 in., don't cut them or try to plane the entire amount off. Not only is this difficult to do, but you will also wind up creating a twisted plane, making it nearly impossible for the casing to lie flat. In most cases, you're

better off leaving the jambs as they are, installing the casing, and trying to fill the gap between the edge of the casing and the wall with a feathered skim coat of drywall compound.

Measuring jamb extensions

To determine the width of the jamb extensions, hold a straightedge on the wall so that it spans the corner of the window opening. Measure from the straightedge to the window frame and add $1/16$ in. This means the jamb will extend ever so slightly into the room, making it easier to apply the casing.

It's common for a window to be slightly out of parallel with the plane of the wall, so measure all four corners with a straightedge. If the measurements differ by more than $3/16$ in., then I custom-cut the extensions, tapering them slightly to match the true dimensions. If the width of the jamb extensions differs by less than $3/16$ in., I split the difference and adjust the discrepancy with the casing. That is, I cut all jamb extensions $3/32$ in. narrower than the widest piece. This means that at the deepest corner, the jamb extension dips $3/32$ in.; at the shallowest corner, it protrudes $3/32$ in. Typically, I can make up for this later by rolling the casing in slightly where the jamb dips and caulking between the casing and the wall where it protrudes.

Ripping jamb extensions to width

I mill jamb extensions from S4S stock (boards that are sanded smooth on all four sides), typically Eastern white pine, and use the same material for the window frame. Choose the best grade your budget will allow. I prefer using clear material rather than trying to conceal knots, which are hard to seal and which sometimes loosen or fall out. Because of the way that light from the

PRO TIP

Don't assume that the window is in the same plane as the wall. Check carefully with a straightedge at all four corners.

WHAT CAN GO WRONG

When the windows and walls are out of whack by more than $3/32$ in., I scribe the jamb extensions to fit and rip each piece to width with a jigsaw. I rip slightly wider than the mark so there is enough extra to plane off the saw marks; otherwise, these will show at the reveal.

SAFETY FIRST

A tablesaw is a dangerous machine. Always keep blades sharp and clean. Only raise the blade a tooth height higher than the thickness of the stock you are cutting. Use push sticks and keep your hands away from the blade, even when making a closed cut. Always push cut pieces all the way through the cut and clear of the blade.

window falls across the jambs, any surface blemish will likely show up, even through paint.

Always cut your jambs from solid wood, not MDF or plywood. Composite materials tend to split when nailed or screwed through the edge. For narrow, square-edged extension pieces, I try to plan my rips so I have a factory-milled edge facing into the room. For example, if I am ripping $1\frac{3}{8}$-in.-wide pieces, I cut them from 1x4 stock. With each pass through the tablesaw, I hold one factory edge toward the fence. This way, each piece has one clean edge that doesn't require planing away the saw marks, which would otherwise be seen along the reveal.

Picture-frame assembly

Using a small square or a reveal block, I first mark the edge of the window jamb for the reveal. This provides precise marks from which to measure the length of each extension.

If the extensions are less than 1 in. wide, I cut each piece to length, and then nail it directly to the window with 6d to 8d nails, depending on the width of the extension. Nail both sides of each corner and every 10 in. to 12 in. in between. When nailing, be sure to drive the nails straight (in line with the existing window jamb), not angled toward the window, to avoid blowouts.

If the extensions are wider than 1 in., I find it's always worthwhile to preassemble the four jambs. I lay the pieces out on a piece of plywood or large benchtop and screw the corners together. It is then much easier to nail the entire assembly to the window jamb rather than aligning and installing each piece separately.

Traditional-trim assembly

If the window has a stool, I cut and install this piece first, as described below. If the extensions are wide, the stool can be built right into the jamb assembly and installed as a unit.

The stool should be installed as level as possible with stable shims below it. If something heavy is set on the stool (or worse, someone stands on it when hanging curtains), the stool must bear considerable weight. The stool can split or sag if it's not well shimmed.

Cutting a window stool Making a window stool requires several steps.

1. The first thing to determine is the width of the stool. To do this, hold a straightedge across the lower corners of the window and measure the distance from the window to the straightedge. But instead of ripping to this width, you need to add the thickness of the casing, plus another ¾ in. This means the stool will protrude beyond the plane of the casing by ¾ in. This added dimension may be larger if a wider window stool is preferred. I think a ¾-in. projection looks best. If you are using a back band or building up casing from several overlapping pieces of material, make sure you account for the added thickness when figuring the width of the stool. When you know the overall width, rip the stool out of a piece of 5/4 stock (see the illustration on p. 48).

Making Wide Extension Jambs

WIDER EXTENSIONS require three passes through a tablesaw.

1. I first rip the material to width, just as I do for narrow stock. Here again, I try to keep a factory edge facing the room.

2. Then, I rip a step in the back of each piece. Ripping this step, or shoulder, requires two passes through the tablesaw. The first pass is made with the board on edge and the blade set at an angle (the angle depends on the depth of the extension piece you are cutting). The height of the blade should be set so it reaches from the outside corner of the board to the inside corner of your second cut **A**.

3. The second pass cuts the back face. This cut should be made about 1 in. from the edge that will butt against the window or so that it reaches the kerf made by the first pass **B**. Set the height of the blade at about ⅜ in. for 1x stock, so the blade reaches to the middle of the board. Keep the blade vertical. This completes the step **C**.

2. Cut the stool to length. The total length of the stool must account for the width of the window (including any jamb extension reveals), the casing reveals on both sides, the width of the casing on both sides, plus an additional ¾ in. beyond each casing end. I usually rip the edge that will butt to the window with a very slight 2-degree bevel. This back cut ensures that the stool meets tightly against the window.

MEASURING A WINDOW STOOL

Jamb extension

Casing

Window unit

Extension width

¾-in. projection

Casing width

¼-in. casing reveal

¼-in. jamb reveal

Inside width of window unit

Casing thickness

¾-in. projection

Window stool width = extension width + casing width + ¾-in. projection
Window stool length = inside window unit + 2(jamb reveal) + 2(casing reveal) + 2(casing) + 2(projection)

On some open-grain hardwoods, such as oak and mahogany, the end grain may be visually quite different. In that case, it's better to cut a miter return than to simply round over the end. Be sure to leave the stool horns long, so that you have plenty of stock to cut the return blocks with a matching grain.

3. After cutting the sill stock to length and width, round over the outside edge and the ends using a router. I typically use a ½-in. roundover bit for 5/4 stock. Depending on the trim style, you may wish to cut a different profile. Victorian trim, for example, often calls for an ogee edge profile. A more contemporary design, on the other hand, may call for simply easing the edges slightly with a block plane. After shaping the edges, smooth them with sandpaper. If the trim will be painted, prime both sides of the stool.

4. Now you are ready to cut the horns on the ends of the stool. I start by marking the center of the window and the center of the stool piece that has been cut to length. Then,

I draw a centerline across the bottom of the rough opening, so that I can align the stool to this mark and hold it against the wall in its exact location. Measure the distance between the window and the stool piece on both sides of the window to be sure the stool and the window are parallel. If they are, scribe the ends for the horns **A**. If the window is slightly out of parallel with the wall, shim one end of the stool stock. Set the width of a scribe tool (such as a compass) to the distance between the window and the edge of the stool, and then scribe the ends.

5. Finally, hold a square along the inside of the rough opening to mark the inside corners of the horns **B**. I make the cuts for the horns with a miter saw **C** and finish the cut in the corner with a short handsaw. Once the stool is cut, I test-fit it **D**. This may require scribing, both against the window and along the horns **E**. When it fits tight to both the window and the wall, I build it into my extension assembly **F**.

Installing a jamb/sill assembly Before installing the assembly in the window opening, I drill pilot holes through the shoulder of the stepped extension stock and at an angle through the bottom of the stool. These pilot holes keep the jamb extensions and stool from splitting when the screws are driven home. The pilot holes also allow me to get the right angle, so that the screw doesn't burst through the inside of the window frame.

1. Install the extension assembly with 1½-in.-long screws **A** (see the photo on p. 50). I use a long Phillips bit in a magnetic holder to reach between the assembly and the drywall. This can be a pretty tight squeeze, and sometimes

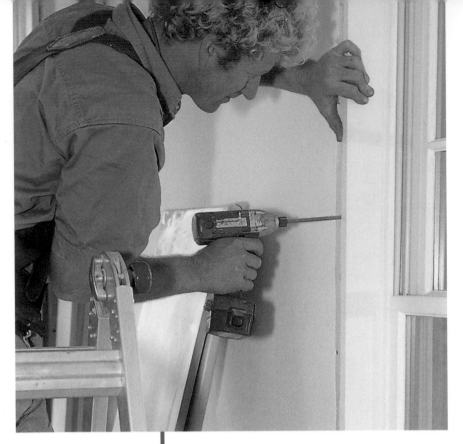

A jamb with a step ripped into it can be installed with screws.

3. Nail through the sill with 8d to 10d finish nails. As a last step, nail through the face of the horns into the trimmer studs below with a 10d nail in each side. Be sure to predrill the holes before nailing to prevent splitting the horn.

Picture-Framing a Window

A picture-frame window has four pieces of casing, each mitered at 45 degrees in the corners. The challenge here is to get all four miters tight. This depends on having a perfectly square window.

One way to check a window for square is by holding a framing square inside the jamb at each corner. However, a better way is to measure and compare the diagonals across the window. If the two diagonals are unequal, the window is out of square and you should try to correct it, if possible, by forcing in new shims around the window. If you can't do that, you may be able to compensate by making adjustments to the reveal width and the miters. Correcting for an out-of-square window requires patience and experience. Just remember that all the miters are connected; an adjustment to one will affect all the others.

Layout

The casing lines up on the edge of the window jamb (or jamb extension) about ¼ in. in from the inside corner. This ¼ in. is the reveal. Begin your layout by using a small tri-square to measure and mark the jambs for a consistent reveal, as follows:

1. Adjust the blade to a short ¼ in.

2. Hold a pencil at the end of the blade. Some carpenters file a notch at the end to hold the pencil, but it's fine just to hold the pencil tight to the end of the blade.

PRO TIP

Make sure a window stool is well shimmed below. Sometimes it must bear considerable weight.

---

even the magnetic bit holder is too wide. You may want to use a hex extension bit from a screw gun, which is easier to maneuver in tight spaces. One screw near the corners and every 16 in. in between is sufficient to hold the assembly securely in place.

2. Be sure to secure the sill, too. Begin by shimming under it. Typically, the gap between a finish sill and the rough framing is quite wide, so I usually cut strips of plywood to use as shims. Stack these and slip a couple of new shims on top, and then snugly wedge the entire stack into the opening. Just make sure you don't shim too much. It's rather easy to bow the sill upward when pushing wedged shims together. Depending on the width of the window, a stack of shims should be located in one or two places in the middle, as well as below each side jamb (though sometimes the side jambs of a window unit extend hard to the rough sill, so this isn't always necessary).

3. Move the square and pencil down the length of the window jamb, scribing a line parallel to the edge **A**.

These marks tell you where to nail the casing. You don't have to make a continuous line. The most important thing is to mark at the corners and somewhere in the middle of each length. In fact, I have made the mistake of marking a continuous line for the reveal on unpainted trim, and then regretted it. After the casing was nailed on, I could see my line in most places, and it proved very difficult to erase.

Measuring length

Begin by holding a long piece of casing stock across the head of the window, lining it up along the edge of the jamb on the reveal marks. Make a mark on the casing at the reveal mark in each corner. This marks the inside, or short point, of the miter. (The outside corner of the miter is called the long point.) Make a slash across the casing to indicate the direction of miter cut from

short point to long point, so that you don't lose track when you make the cut **B**.

On a production job, you would repeat this procedure for the other three sides before installing the pieces. However, if the windows aren't perfectly square, or if you anticipate other problems, start by just laying out and cutting the two angles on the head casing first. Then tack it in place and continue measuring and cutting the remaining pieces one at a time. This way, if the miters are wildly off, you can hold rough-cut lengths directly over the tacked-up head casing and mark the actual short and long points of each angle. Doing this takes patience and skill, but if you keep the casing long, you can often sneak up on it.

Cutting miter joints

If you're new to cutting miters, a picture-frame window is a good place to practice. You can use a wood miter box or a power miter saw. I usually use a miter saw, which is faster and makes it

PRO TIP

Make sure you don't shim too much. It's rather easy to bow the sill upward when pushing wedged shims together.

TRADE SECRET

Trim carpentry requires the utmost accuracy. For the most precise measurements, don't use the hook end of a tape measure. Instead, start your measurements at the 1-in. mark (and be sure to subtract 1 in. from the tape reading). This method is called "cutting the one" or "burning an inch."

easier to precisely adjust an angle if a window frame is not perfectly square.

1. Cut the two miters on the head piece first, and then tack this piece in place (without sinking the nails home).

2. Cut matching side pieces and tack them in place, securing them at the top ends only.

3. Cut the bottom piece. Before making final miter cuts, measure between the long points on the two side pieces, and then double-check the short-point measurements.

Nailing

When you know all the pieces are the right length and the miters are cut at the right angles, you can finish driving your tack nails home. For standard clamshell casing, I use 4d (1½-in.-long) nails along the thinner inside edges into

Constructing a Wood Miter Box

BEFORE POWER MITER SAWS were commonly available, trim carpenters relied on a simple miter box made from scrap lumber and a sharp handsaw. It's a nice jig to have on hand when setting up the miter saw and spewing dust seem like overkill.

1. Make a basic box using 1x4 hardwood for the sides and a scrap of 2x6 framing lumber for the bottom. Screw the sides to the bottom, making sure all the parts are flat, square, and parallel.

2. Find the center and mark across the top of both sides.

3. Measure the inside width of the box. Make a mark on both sides of the centerline the same distance as the width of the box. (Your marks should make a square.)

4. With a square and a pencil, draw three cutlines down from the marks; the center will be for square cuts and the other two for 45-degree cuts. Draw these inside the box and then extend them to the outside.

5. Tack a piece of scrap 1x2 alongside one of the angled lines, as shown. Use this to guide a handsaw as you cut three slots—one at the centerline and one at each of the 45-degree angles.

6. Use the slots to make square and mitered cuts.

I. Make a Basic Box

1x4 (hardwood)

2x6

2. Mark the Centerline

Align the framing square on the centerline.

Framing square

3. Mark the Cut Lines

Same as inside width

Diagonals
Centerline

4. Extend the Lines Inside the Box

Extend the square lines down the inside edges.

5. Cut Along the Lines

Tack on a guide strip.

6. Use the Miter Box

Crosscut handsaw

Not all miters are a perfect 45°. Use this geometrical layout for odd angles or to create a miter for an out-of-square opening.

1. Ideally, right-angled miters are 45 degrees each.

2. With a compass, swing an arc from AA to BB and from AA to CC. Any radius that is greater than the width of the molding will do.

3. Next, swing arcs from BB and CC to create an X. The line drawn from this X to AA and through the joint bisects the angle. Transfer it with a bevel gauge and set the chopsaw.

the window jamb and larger 6d (2-in.-long) nails along the thicker edges into the trimmer studs beneath the drywall. I typically pair nails at about 45 degrees along the trim, mirroring the pair near the miters. I finish by driving a 4d nail along the outside edge of the casings near the long points of each miter. Make sure you set the nails with a nail set and fill the holes afterward.

Traditional Casing

Casing for a traditional stool-and-apron window always has a few less miters than a picture-frame window; sometimes, it has no miters at all. Nevertheless, when you factor in the extra time involved in cutting and fitting the stool, traditional trim takes more time to install.

Mitered casing

One of the simplest traditional trim styles uses standard colonial casing stock mitered at the head (see the illustration on p. 54). If the window is square, it is easy to do.

Removing Nails

INSTEAD OF USING a hammer claw to pull out finish nails, I usually use a pair of end nippers. These bite easily into the nail shank at any point. Whenever possible, I try to pull the nail out from the back. The finish head pulls right through the material, resulting in a clean finish surface. This works especially well when disassembling woodwork that will be reinstalled.

When nailing near the end of a board, blunt the nail's tip to prevent it from splitting the wood. This can be done quickly by holding the nail upside down and striking the tip with a few blows of a hammer.

Mitered   Butt Joint   Built-Up Casing

The Right Insulation

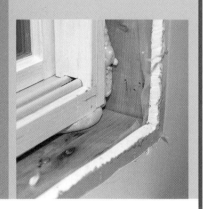

1. Cut the two side pieces. Measure the distance from the top of the stool to the reveal line across the head jamb **A**. With mitered casing, this length will give you the short point of the miters.

2. Cut the head casing. To find the length, first tack the two side casings in place, and then rough-cut a piece of casing for the head. Hold this piece over the window and mark the long points of the miters directly off the side casings.

If the window is slightly out of square, I prefer to cut the head casing first, measuring between the reveal marks on each side to find the short points for the miter cuts on each end of the head piece. I then tack the head piece in place and rough-cut the side pieces to length. This way I can lay my side pieces right over the head casing to mark the long and short points of each miter for a perfect fit, similar to the method for picture-framing a window.

Butt joints

Generally, when I fit traditional stool-and-apron trim, I don't cut any miters at all. I typically use "flat stock"—standard 1x4 or wider finish lumber—and join the head casing to the side casings with a butt joint. In this case, the side casings butt square against the bottom edge of the head casing (see the illustration above).

Fixing Bad Miters

THE ANGLES ARE OFF

If the opening is not perfectly square, a miter can be open at the heel or at the point. Correct this by recutting the angle on a miter saw. The adjustment may only be half a degree or so, and it may be difficult to set the saw at this angle. Instead, consider using wedges between the casing and the saw table (see the top photo at right). Remember: Recutting the angle will change the length of your material, so always check the window for square. Cut some test miters until you get the angles right.

THE VERTICAL IS OFF

A miter can also be open if the wall is not perfectly flat. To tighten up the joint, back-cut the miter slightly. Very slight gaps can be shaved with a low-angle block plane or filed down with a rasp. More extreme gaps can be back-cut with a miter saw by propping the casing up on the table.

THE SURFACE PLANE IS OFF

If the wall is not flat and the window is cocked, the top surfaces of the two pieces may not meet perfectly even though the gap is tight. In this case, carefully shave down the casing with a chisel or shim one piece slightly forward (see the photo at right). If you shim the casing forward, caulk the gap before painting.

PRO TIP

Use a biscuit in the butt joints on casings. A biscuit helps align the joint, making it stronger and less likely to open up over time.

WHAT CAN GO WRONG

Butt joints may not fit perfectly if the window jamb isn't perfectly flush with the surface of the wall or if the wall or the trim material is warped. For example, if the jamb protrudes slightly, the head casing may tip back slightly, opening a gap at the joint. Try either back-cutting the end of each side casing or shimming the head casing slightly forward.

The biggest advantage of butt joints is that if the wood dries and shrinks, the joint can be tightened back up. Miters, on the other hand, can't be tightened up later because the wood shrinks unevenly across the joint, changing the miter angle (remember that wood shrinks at different rates lengthwise and crosswise to the grain).

When using butt joints, I usually start with the side casing.

1. Measure the length of side casings from the top of the stool to the reveal mark across the head jamb.

2. After cutting the side pieces to length, tack them in place.

3. Measure the distance across the top of the window, from the outside of one side to the outside of the other. This is the length of the head casing. I usually cut the head casing square at this dimension. However, some carpenters prefer to let the head casing overhang the sides by a small amount—usually the same amount at which the horns project, or about ¾ in. In this case, add 1½ in. to the length of the head piece (or simply use the same measurement as that of the stool) before cutting square.

4. Once the head casing fits, nail it in place along the jamb edge first, then along the top edge. Space the nails 10 in. to 12 in. apart and slope the nails at a slight downward angle to drive the head piece tightly into the butt joints. Later, if the framing and trim shrink and the butt joint opens up, you can tighten the joint by hammering against a block.

Fitting an apron

The apron should be cut from the same width stock as the casing. However, it doesn't need to be cut from the same material. In fact, it's common for the apron to be cut from profiled stock, even when the casing is cut from flat stock. Find the length of the apron by measuring the distance from one outside edge of the casing to the other. This measurement should be the same length as the head piece, if the head doesn't project past the side pieces.

If the apron is cut from flat stock, simply center the apron below the window stool and nail it in place with 8d nails every 10 in. If the apron is wide, you may only have nailing along the top edge. I usually plane (with a block plane) the top edge of the apron so that it fits tightly

to the stool **A**. I like to clamp the edge with a Quik-clamp® to draw the stool and apron together, then drive a few 8d finish nails to secure them **B**.

If the apron is cut from profiled stock, the ends must be visually "closed," and you will have to cut miter returns. In that case, the length of the apron runs from long point to long point, with very short triangular pieces of stock meeting at the miters and returning to the wall.

Built-up casings

As the name implies, many pieces of casing can be matched and layered to build up ornate, extra-wide trim profiles. Use your imagination to combine stock moldings, but keep in mind that every piece you add doubles the installation time.

Built-up casing typically includes a "ground" made of flat stock, with a variety of trim pieces layered over the ground to create complexity. Make sure you account for the added dimensions in both thickness and width before ripping your stool stock.

I always cut short pieces of all the layers and make a model to figure out how they will fit together. Then I measure the built-up dimensions directly off the model.

Built-up moldings can be simple bands applied over flat stock to create an ornate capital or a more elaborate layered casing. An example of a more elaborate built-up casing includes a ground of S4S 1x4, which is installed with butt joints like a conventional casing.

1. After cutting, fitting, and installing the ground (holding it to the reveal line on the window jamb), a secondary molding cut from 1¼-in. by ⅜-in. ogee doorstop is layered on top. The ogee aligns to the outside edge of the ground, laps over the butt joints, and is mitered across the head. The built-up casing is now 1⅛ in. thick.

2. After cutting and installing the overlay molding, a cove molding is installed around the outside edge of the ground. This ⅞-in. piece covers up the lap joint between the ground and the overlaying molding. Once it is installed, the total width of each side casing is 4⅜ in.

3. Use 4d finish nails to secure overlay pieces to the ground **C**. There's no need to drive through the ground into the trimmer studs. This is a good place to use a pneumatic brad nailer, if you have one **D**.

Unless your ground lies perfectly flat, you may see significant gaps between the overlay moldings and the underlying trim. Butt joints may need to be belt-sanded if the head and side pieces of the ground are significantly out of alignment. However, if the trim will be painted, a judicious bead of caulk goes a long way toward hiding minor defects.

BUILT-UP CASING

Cove

Ogee stop

Jamb

1✕4 "ground"

1⅛ in.

1⅞ in.

Stool

4⅜ in.

C

D

DESIGN
OPTIONS

▲ The heads of doors and windows should be treated consistently. The simple capitals shown here have a bead joint along the bottom of the head casing with a profiled molding capping the top. The capitals project as far as the window stools, a reserved treatment echoed in the simple newel caps.

▲ This composition of windows surrounding a door is trimmed out with a built-up casing. An applied molding at the outside edge of the casing frames the large composition, while a flat casing with a beaded edge surrounds each opening. The window stool laps the door casing, and the apron integrates with the wall panel.

▲ Symmetry rules in a gable end with three windows. The higher head of the center window uses a simple capital. The head trim of the two side windows overlaps slightly onto the side casing of the center window—a tiny but elegant detail for resolving these intersections.

▲ With its simple capital and profiled stool, this accent window keeps the focus on the stained glass. The ends of the stool project much farther than you would typically see—a small but flamboyant gesture that seems to echo the stained-glass design.

◀ Sometimes subtle choices make all the difference: Note how the divider between the shelf and the window serves as the left-hand side of the window casing, while the left-hand side of the bookcase dies into the wall. You could use the same narrow-size trim for both places, which would create a more symmetrical frame around the shelf and window. But this asymmetrical pairing nicely draws the composition into the corner, which balances with the window seat below, creating a more intimate reading nook.

RUNNING BASEBOARD

1 Baseboard Layout p. 62

2 Cutting Baseboard p. 66

3 Installing Baseboard p. 71

When it comes time to install baseboard, old-time carpenters gladly yield to younger members of the crew—the ones quickest at getting up and down from the floor and the ones least likely to complain about crawling around the job site on hands and knees.

Baseboard—also called mopboard, skirting, or simply base—should be one of the last pieces of trim to install. After the door casings have been installed, the heating vents and electrical outlets roughed in, the drywall taped, and the floors sanded, baseboard ties it all together. As the name suggests, it provides a visual base for the vertical, or "standing," trim, such as door casing and wainscoting. But it's much more than a decorative band. Baseboard hides the inevitable gap between the wall and floor, and it covers the all-important space around the perimeter of a wood floor that allows floorboards to expand and contract. ▶ ▶ ▶

Baseboard Layout

One-piece baseboard can be run quite quickly, but it isn't very forgiving of sags and dips in the floor and walls. If you're working in an old house, plan at the very least to run an additional shoe molding to conform to discrepancies in the floor. Thinner one-piece base stock will bend enough to conform to an uneven wall surface. But if you're running a tall, traditional base, plan on using a separate base cap as well.

Regardless of the material you use, work out how the base will intersect with the door casing and stairways well in advance. These are details that you want to work out when you're installing the door casing, not running the baseboard.

Begin the baseboard layout by defining the areas in the house where the baseboard will be most visible, and then sort through your material. Cull through the pile, tagging the best-looking lengths for the most conspicuous areas. The entry, living, and dining areas typically receive the best material, while hallways and bedrooms receive less-than-perfect lengths. The worst material—pieces with large knots or slightly twisted, bowed, or crooked lengths—can be cut into smaller pieces for use in closets and behind radiators.

BASEBOARD TYPES

Wood baseboard comes in a wide variety of styles and sizes. Choose a design best suited to your particular situation.

Small Base (or Sanitary)
The baseboard equivalent to clamshell: This small rounded profile is thin enough to bend, conforming easily to walls, and on long runs even bowing to fill small dips in the floor.

Profiled One-Piece Base
This can add elegance to an interior trim package but is not very forgiving of wavy walls and sagging floors. Save this option for use in new construction, when you know the walls will be reasonably straight and flat and the floors level.

Tall Base with Base Shoe
In older houses, opt for a three-piece baseboard. While the main piece stays rigid, the flexible cap conforms to waves in the wall and the thin shoe mold bends to match sags in the floor.

Finish wall w/finished edge

Blocking

Reveal

Base flush w/finish wall

Flush Base
This looks simple but is deceivingly difficult to install. The backer must be continuous, the framing plates must be even, and the bottom edge of the drywall must be level and finished with J-bead.

Installation order

To run baseboard efficiently, start with a room survey to determine a logical order for installing it (see the sidebar on p. 64). Look at all the corners and note the inside and outside ones. Outside corners will be mitered, so these should be done first, if possible. All inside corners of profiled base should be coped. (Coping is not necessary for square-edged baseboard.)

Accommodating Out-of-Square Casing or Plinths

IF A DOOR CASING or plinth block is out of square relative to the baseboard, you may be able to scribe the cut. Most of the time, however, the length of baseboard fits into a corner, so you don't have any room to run the baseboard long while scribing. In this case, you have two options: a bevel square or a "preacher block." The bevel square works best if you can hold it on a piece of scrap baseboard instead of on the floor.

If you have several of these cuts to make, you can save time by making a preacher block. Run the baseboard long past the door casing, then slip this U-shaped block over the baseboard and trace the exact line of the cut.

BASE MEETS DOOR

Well before you start running baseboard, you must work out the details of where it will intersect the door casing. Above all, make sure the baseboard does not project farther from the wall than the door casing.

Flush

Baseboard flush with door casing

Shoe molding trimmed at an angle laps onto casing.

Reveal

3/4-in. baseboard butts 5/4 door casing.

Plinth Block

3/4-in. door casing

5/4 plinth block

3/4-in. baseboard

Back Band

Baseboard butts into thicker back band.

PRO TIP

Coping a molding with a profile is better than using an inside miter. A coped joint will shrink and expand less with seasonal changes.

Efficient Baseboard Layout

EFFICIENT BASEBOARD layout is mostly about the sequence in which you work your way around a room. Start on the wall opposite the main entrance to a room, and then work from each end around the other sides of the room, as shown in the illustration at right. Arrange the cuts so that the joints are not in a direct line of sight. Work from long lengths to shorter lengths. *(The letters on the photos below correspond to the letters on the illustration at right.)*

Start baseboard installation on longest wall opposite entry.

A. Base to door casing.

B. Inside corner at door casing.

C. Outside corner.

D. Inside corner.

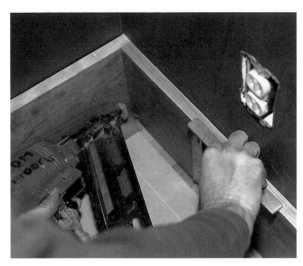

In a butt joint for baseboard, both pieces are cut square. The lap piece (left) is installed first, and the meeting piece (right) butts into it.

Start on the wall opposite the main entrance to a room, and then work from each end around each side of the room. The goal is to arrange the cuts so that the joints are out of your direct line of sight. If possible, avoid looking "into" a joint.

I call the first piece installed the lap piece. This length is cut square on both ends and laps behind the butt (or coped) ends of the meeting pieces (see the photo above). Ideally, you want to start on one of the longest walls with this first piece. Since both ends are cut square, you're less likely to spoil a long piece of stock by cutting a bad cope.

Accurate measurements

The most efficient approach is to first measure as many runs as possible, cut those pieces all at once, and then install them.

1. Start by identifying any outside corners and plan to measure and cut these first. I start by rough-cutting the board to length, butting it hard to the wall in one corner, and letting it run past the outside corner on the other.

This way, I can mark the bevel for the outside corner directly off the wall. It's always better to have the opposite end abut the wall rather than butt another piece of baseboard. This allows for some adjustment in length in case the outside corner bevel needs to be adjusted to fit precisely.

2. Next, measure all the lap pieces that have square cuts on both ends, bending the tape into the corner. For long runs, cut the board $\frac{1}{16}$ in. longer than the measured length. The length will have to be bowed slightly to be fit into place but can be easily pushed against the wall. Don't cut it too long, however, or you may crack the drywall tape in the corner when the piece is pushed into place.

3. To measure the meeting pieces, hold a scrap of baseboard in the corner and trace its profile onto the wall **A**. Then measure to the pencil line of the profile **B** (on p. 66). This will be the short point for the cope on the meeting piece, so be sure to add the thickness of the board to the cut length. Take care during this initial measuring phase to check the tilt of the baseboard. If the wall is out of plumb or

A

B

Cutting Baseboard

Although it would seem logical that most baseboard is simply cut square or at 45-degree angles, I find that this is rarely the case. More often, cuts vary to conform to the irregularities of the walls and the particular type of baseboard stock you're using. Most of these cuts can be made easily by hand with a power circular saw and a simple coping saw. But I've found that a power miter saw speeds the task and vastly improves the quality of my cuts.

Butt joints

In theory, butt ends are cut square. But to allow for some relief from the mud buildup in corners, I always back-cut the butt ends of my lap pieces slightly by about 1 degree to 2 degrees. I often undercut the lap ends, too, making a slight angle in the board to allow room for mud buildup at the bottom of the corner. Remember: The lap piece only needs to fit tightly into the corner at the top; the bottom will be covered by the coped joint (see the top left photo on the facing page).

I rarely back-cut the meeting ends—those that butt the lap pieces (or coped pieces, if the baseboard has a profile). However, I often overcut or undercut the piece if the lap piece is tipped in or out. Before making your final cut, double-check the corner with a Speed Square on the

there is a heavy buildup of drywall mud at the base of a corner joint, the baseboard will tip back. Unless you take this into account, you'll end up with an ugly gap in the corners.

To avoid creating corner gaps, I make it a habit to quickly check for square when measuring with scrap pieces. Hold a Speed Square® against the floor. If the base is more than 1/8 in. out of plumb, make a note to cut the meeting piece at a slight angle to match. If it is close to square but not exact, go ahead and cut the meeting piece square, then push the joint tight with a flat bar, as described below (see "Nailing" on pp. 71–74).

4. There will always be a few pieces to measure after you have some base pieces installed. One common example is a length that is coped on one end and precisely butted into the door casing on the other. In this case, cut the cope first, leaving the end long, and then come back later with a preacher block to mark the cutline for the butt end.

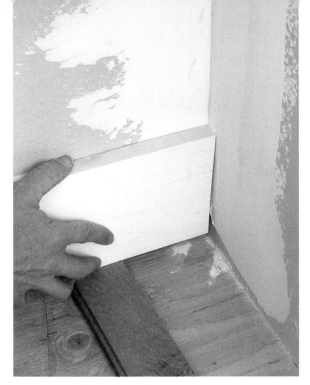

If a heavy buildup of drywall mud prevents the baseboard from fitting snugly in the inside corner, the first piece of baseboard in a corner (called the lap piece) can be undercut, as shown above. This way, only the top edge—the only part that will show—contacts the wall.

floor. If the wall is tipped so that the baseboard pieces do not fit square when held flat against the wall, measure the difference off square and cut the lap piece at a slight angle to match.

Miter outside corners

Outside corners of rooms rarely end up being perfect 90-degree angles. Even though the corner may be perfectly framed, metal corner bead and the joint compound covering it conspire to make the angle either fatter or leaner. I find that most of the time the outside miter on each run of baseboard must be cut at an angle slightly greater than 45 degrees.

1. To find the exact angle, I draw the corner right on the floor using scrap baseboard stock as a template. If I'm working on a finished floor, I lay down wide masking tape on the floor and make marks on that.

2. Take a rough length of baseboard and hold it against the wall, letting it run past the corner. Draw a line on the floor along the bottom edge to mark the outside face of the baseboard **A**. Do this on both sides of the corner, so that the two lines intersect **B**. Position the baseboard stock. Cut or cope the inside corner end so that you can hold the baseboard tightly in place. With the end running long, past the outside corner, mark the face of the board where the floor marks intersect **C**. Then mark the top edge of the board where it touches the corner of the wall. Since corner bead is slightly rounded

TRADE SECRET

In any kind of carpentry work, one thing that will slow you down is constantly changing your saw settings. Try to avoid this by planning ahead and grouping the different types of cuts together. For example, first cut all the back-cut butt joints with a 1-degree or 2-degree angle going in one direction. Next, cut the ones going in the other direction. Then cut all the reverse miters for your cope joints.

PROTIP

Since cutting baseboard often requires some trial and error to fit the joints, it's always best to cut a little long and sneak up to the fit.

Ending Baseboard

OCCASIONALLY, IT'S NECESSARY to terminate baseboard at the end of a run. In that case, cut miter returns on the ends of both the baseboard and the base cap. Take care when cutting these tiny miter returns on a power miter box, as the small piece you want tends to fly up into the blade guard or, worse, straight at you. I find it works best to cut the miter first, and then adjust the saw for a straight cut. Glue and miter the return piece to a matching miter on the run of the baseboard or base cap.

on the corner, give yourself some room on this second mark—at least a fat 1/16 in. from where the back of the baseboard touches the wall.

3. The two marks you have made on the baseboard define the limits of your outside bevel cut, but you have a couple of options on how to cut it.

If you're reasonably sure that the corner is plumb, use a Speed Square to draw a line across the face of the baseboard from the floor mark, then connect the line on the top edge with the wall mark. This defines your bevel, which may or may not be 45 degrees, for the long point of the outside miter **D**.

Using a bevel square, draw a miter from the outside corner line (long point of miter) to the mark on the top edge that indicates the wall corner (short point of miter) **E**. Set the bevel angle of your saw to this angle.

If the corner is reasonably square but not plumb, hold your board on the table of the miter saw. Lift the board slightly as you eyeball the two marks until they line up with the blade. Hold the board at this elevation and shim it up on the miter-saw table to hold it there, then cut.

Chances are good that your outside corner is neither plumb nor square, and so you will probably want to try some variation of these options, such as drawing the square line across the face of the baseboard, tipping it ever so slightly off plumb, eyeballing it, and then cutting it. If the top edge is covered by base cap, you can also cheat by cutting the baseboards slightly long, so that you are out from the bum corner. If you're far enough away, the baseboard fits when cut at a perfect square and bevel. A little experience (meaning lots of trial and error) will help you find the right solution.

Block Corners

ONE NICE ALTERNATIVE to inside or outside corners for baseboard is corner blocks. When I've used them, I've typically cut them from 5/4 stock to make a 1⅛-in. by ⅛-in. square block (or peg). The advantage is that the baseboard abuts each side, which creates a much more forgiving corner than a miter for tall baseboard, especially if the house lines are out of whack. I've also used a thicker 2x2 block on bullnose wall corners. For this detail, I first gingerly cut out the drywall bullnose and corner bead (usually a PVC corner bead) with a sharp utility knife. This allows me to partially bury the block in the corner of the wall (and it inevitably needs touching up with drywall mud). The result, however, is much more satisfying, I think, than trying to wrap the corner with two 22.5-degree miters, which is what I usually see done.

Corner blocks on both the inside and the outside aren't affected by shrinkage or differential movement and offer an alternative to cope and miter joints when running baseboard.

Inside Block Corner

Outside Block Corner

Cope inside corners

Unless the trim style calls for corner blocks, I always cope inside corners when the baseboard has a profile. Coping has two clear advantages over an inside miter. First, a coped joint is very forgiving of out-of-square corners and irregular wall surfaces, so it's easy to cut a tight joint at the outset. Second, a cope stays tight over time. Unlike a miter, which tends to open and close with changes in humidity, a coped joint can only open if the lap piece shrinks in thickness (perpendicular to the grain) or if the meeting piece shrinks lengthwise (along the grain). In both cases, this type of shrinkage is minimal.

1. Reverse the bevel. Start with a reverse-bevel cut—a 45-degree bevel with the long point on the back of the board **A**. Overcut the length for this bevel by a healthy ¹⁄₁₆ in. so that the piece will be slightly long and the leading edge of the coped profile will bite into the piece of wood it meets. If you know the lap piece is tipped in or out, scribe the

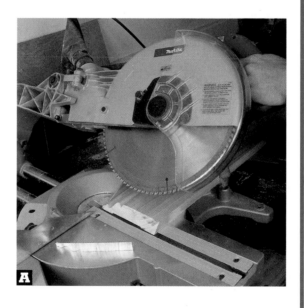

angle first, then cut the bevel to that line (a compound angle).

2. After cutting the reverse bevel for a cope, make a few straight chops in a power miter saw to clear away the bulk of the material **B**. This makes it easier to maneuver the coping saw around the turns of a tight profile.

B

C

D

E

3. Mark the edge. The reverse bevel defines the profile you will remove; however, the actual joint is really closer to a butt joint. Therefore, I use a small tri-square to mark the square that will butt into the piece of baseboard lapped behind **C**. I may still back-cut beyond this square line, but it gives me a reference at the edge.

4. Trace the profile. With the flat side of a pencil, blacken the line of the profile **D**. This helps define it, making it much easier to follow while you are sawing the wood.

5. Rough out with a jigsaw. A coping saw is a rather delicate instrument, and I find it slow and painstaking to use for the long, straight run on one-piece base stock. Instead, I use a jigsaw to rough out the joint **E**. Some carpenters cut the entire joint with a jigsaw, then fine-tune it.

6. Cope. I switch to a coping saw to navigate the twists and turns of the profiled parts of the base stock **F**. Don't force the blade through tight curves. A coping saw works best when it's used delicately. In tight curves, I break the cut into sections, coming at the blackened line from different directions, gradually sneaking up on it until I have a smooth

F

curve. To fine-tune the cut, don't be shy about employing a host of other tools, such as a rat-tail rasp, a piece of sandpaper, and even a utility knife, to carve and smooth the cut.

7. Fit. Getting a tight fit may take a few tries. As you can see in , the lap piece with which the cope mates essentially passes through the coped profile. So when fine-tuning the joint, you must be sure to clear all the material behind the leading edge of the profile. I call the coped edge a "knife edge" to emphasize that the cope has been back-cut. Because I overcut the length by a good $1/16$ in. at the offset, the knife edge actually bites into its mate when the baseboard is snapped into place.

Coping well takes some practice, so be patient. It's particularly challenging with hardwood, but with persistence, you can get a crisp edge that mates precisely. Soft pine cuts easily—sometimes too easily. The resulting edge may end up a little ragged, but if the baseboard is cut slightly long, the joint will still squeeze together tightly.

Installing Baseboard

Ideally, you've cut most of the baseboard to length, so now you're ready to start installing it. Follow the installation order described above (see "Installation Order" on pp. 63–65). I usually start opposite the main entrance with a piece that has two lap ends. As I work around the room, I check the fit before nailing the piece in place. To fit the boards, first tap one piece into place, using a block of wood to protect the baseboard from the hammer, and check the fit against the floor. If you're not using shoe molding, you may need to scribe the bottom edge to conform to an uneven floor. Double-check the fit of each joint as well before nailing it home. There's a lot of trial and error involved when fitting baseboard, so if you're at all uncertain, it's always best to cut a little long and sneak up on the fit.

Nailing

When you're satisfied with the fit, nail the baseboard in place. I start nailing in the middle of a run, leaving the ends loose until I have the meeting pieces in place. This gives me some flexibility if I have to shim the ends for a tighter fit in the corners.

I typically use $2\frac{1}{2}$-in.-long (8d) finish nails for nailing most $5/8$-in.- and $3/4$-in.-thick base stock to walls. For thicker 5/4 stock, I use longer 10d nails. When I'm running low, one-piece baseboard (less than 4 in. tall), I place two nails— one low into the bottom wall plate and another higher into each stud. When I'm running taller, three-piece baseboard, I nail only high (in the top third of the baseboard) into each stud, and then let the shoe molding hold the bottom edge. This helps prevent tall baseboard from cracking, which is likely if it is pinned high and low by a pair of nails.

TRADE SECRET

If you're using a hammer to install trim, always predrill for the nails at the end of a piece to avoid splitting. To predrill, clip the head off a finish nail with a pair of end nippers and chuck the nail into a drill. Use the same size nail for boring the perfect size hole. Only the cuts near the nail points do any work—the rest is friction—so this predrill bit will get pretty hot. In hardwoods, it may even smoke a little. Change the nail/bit frequently to keep it sharp.

Predrill before nailing at the outside corners to avoid splitting the ends.

Nail from both sides of the outside corner and set the nails.

Unless you're using a nailer, predrill holes when nailing near the end of a piece to avoid splitting the wood. I don't worry about splitting when I use a nailer, which shoots a thinner, blunt nail. Hardwood stock is more prone to splitting. Softwood fibers crush together to accommodate a nail, but denser hardwood fibers are pushed aside, increasing the chances that the grain will split all the way through.

Nailing outside miters When predrilling outside miters, don't drill the full length of the nail. Just drill through the first piece and only a short way into the second, so that the combined length of the hole equals about three-fourths of the nail's total length. This ensures that the nail will grab tightly.

When nailing outside miters, I use 4d nails for ⅝-in. stock and 6d nails for ¾-in. stock. I typically use four nails—two from one side and two from the other—to lock the joint in place (see the left photo below). Tall base (over 6 in.) may call for three nails on each side. Small ranch base generally needs only two nails—one on each side.

Nailing inside corners Inside corners need to be nailed only near the corner—two nails in the lap piece and two in the meeting piece. I angle these nails toward the corner to draw the joint together, but the nails are not intended to pass through both pieces of base, only into the wall framing.

As mentioned previously, base can roll back at the corners. This should be taken into account when measuring and cutting the run. When nailing, I always begin in the center of the run, leaving the ends free so I have the option, at the corners, to tip the top of the baseboard forward (a flat bar helps here) so the lap piece butts tightly with a square-cut meeting piece. A few

NAILING THREE-PIECE BASEBOARD

Nail cap to baseboard.

Nail baseboard at the studs.

Stud

Nail shoe molding to the floor.

Finish flooring

Plates

Subfloor

PROTIP

I always glue miter joints with yellow carpenter's glue before nailing them together. This helps keep the joint from opening up.

thin shims behind the corner may be needed to press the joint closed. If slight, a visible gap between the wall and the back of the baseboard can be caulked (or hidden by base cap). However, if the gap is too wide, the meeting piece may need to be recut at an angle to compensate.

Scarf joints Baseboard stock typically comes in 12-ft. to 16-ft. lengths, so it's not difficult to get full-length pieces along most walls. However, in a long hallway (or if you run short on material), it's not uncommon to splice pieces in the middle of a run. For this, you'll want to cut a scarf joint—sometimes called a lapping miter—rather than butt sections together. A scarf joint stays closed better than a simple butt joint should the two lengths of material shrink slightly.

If you're running tall baseboard and have to splice sections together, be sure to break the joint over a stud. This will give you solid backing when you nail the scarf joint together. And before cutting the scarf joint, cut and fit any coped joints or outside miters on the other end

first. This allows you a certain margin for error in case you have to recut the joints.

1. Cut the first miter on one length of baseboard at a 45-degree bevel. The long point of the bevel should be on the back of the baseboard. Position the baseboard on the wall and measure for the matching baseboard piece to the short point on the first piece **A**. This measurement is for the long point of the bevel of the matching piece and will be on

A

Hiding Baseboard Gaps

SHOE MOLDING IS THE best solution for hiding gaps at the bottom of baseboard. However, with one-piece base, there's no way around it—you have to scribe. In this case, tack the baseboard to the wall so that it's level and scribe the bottom edge. If the floor is way out of level, you may have to cheat, holding the baseboard out of level so it doesn't end up too short on one side of the room. The easiest method of scribing to the floor is with a carpenter's pencil. Hold the flat edge of the pencil on the floor, keeping the pencil square to the baseboard.

B

C

D

the face of the board. Cut the miter on the matching piece.

2. Install the first piece. Predrill for the nails and angle the nails so that they are parallel to the open face of the bevel **B**.

3. Glue the open bevel, then install the second piece over it **C**. Using 4d (1-in.) nails, nail directly through the joint perpendicular to the first set. If you don't have a nailer, predrill for the nails. The joint tends to slide around with glue on it, but the predrilled nails make it easier to position the second piece in its exact location **D**.

Base cap and shoe molding

Obviously, base cap and shoe molding must be run after the baseboard is nailed in place. Measuring and cutting is done the same way it was done for the baseboard itself. Inside corners should be coped and outside corners mitered **E**.

If there is a long run that requires a splice, be sure to stagger it so that it doesn't align with a splice in the baseboard. To cut the splice:

1. Install a premitered length to the wall, breaking it over a stud. Measure the second piece from the short point of the bevel on the first piece **F** and cut it to length.

2. After double-checking the fit **G**, put some glue on the joint and nail through the scarf into the stud.

3. Smooth the joint with sandpaper **H**.

E

F

G

H

PRO TIP

To avoid blowouts when using a pneumatic trim nailer, align the nailer in a straight line, sighting along the baseboard.

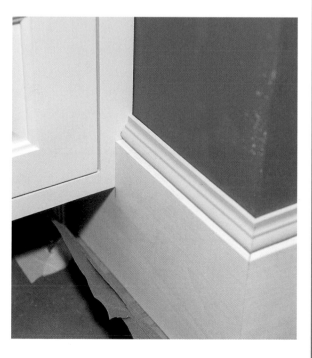

Shoe molding should be nailed only to the floor. Base cap should normally be nailed to the top edge of the baseboard. A 4d nail usually works for both. Do not glue base cap or shoe molding to the baseboard. Each piece should be free to expand and contract at its own rate.

Details

If we only had to deal with outside and inside corners, running baseboard would be a snap. But often there are plenty of niggling details that slow down the job.

Meeting stairs The connection between the stair stringer and the base trim is often one of the most difficult details to work out. Ideally,

When tall baseboard meets a built-in cabinet, the kick space often falls below the top of the baseboard, creating an awkward detail. To avoid this problem, this baseboard has been notched under the kick space, and the base cap dies into a wide cabinet face frame.

Base Meets Stringer

THE FINISH STRINGER on this set of prefab stairs doesn't match the baseboard height specified for the rest of the house. Bob Smith of Housesmith Construction in Burlington, Vermont, resolved the problem this way:

PRO TIP

Locating and cutting
an outlet often requires
painstaking precision.
Be patient and tackle
the job when you've got
enough time to do it right.

1. Position rough stock to mark the length and where the stringer hits the end of the baseboard.

2. Using a tri-square, draw where the stringer line continues across the face of the baseboard up to the profiled cap.

3. Draw a reverse miter for the profiled cap.

4. Cut opposing angles and nail it home. A cap is added over the stringer to meet the reverse miter on the baseboard.

the baseboard and stringer materials should match in thickness and in height. The shoe molding can then overlap the flush joint and return all the way to the first riser. (See "Base Meets Stringer" on p. 76.) If the stringer is thicker than the base stock, you can butt the baseboard, creating a reveal joint. In this case, the shoe molding should be cut at an open miter at the joint instead of continuing to the stair riser.

Dealing with outlets and heat registers
In many older houses, and in some new houses with tall baseboard, it's not uncommon for electrical outlets to be located on the baseboard. In this case, first make sure that the electrical box sticks out far enough to accommodate the extra thickness of the baseboard. Then you'll need to locate and cut the outlet in the baseboard, which often requires painstaking precision.

1. Cut the baseboard to length and lay it face down in front of the outlet. Using a tape measure, transfer the distance from one wall to the centerline of each box, measuring first on the wall and then on the back of the baseboard **A**. Also, measure from the floor to the bottom edge of the box, and then transfer that distance onto the baseboard, measuring from the bottom edge.

2. Find a metal electrical box that is the same size as the one to be installed in the wall and position it on the transfer centerlines **B**. Use the box to mark the exact dimensions for the cut.

3. Use two drill bits. The first is a ⅜-in.-diameter twist bit to bore for the tabs. This allows the outlet to be placed in the metal box after the baseboard and box have been installed. The second is a larger spade bit to

STRINGER INSTALLATION

The base molding meets the skirtboard with a flush or reveal joint. The base shoe may extend to the riser if the base/skirtboard joint is flush.

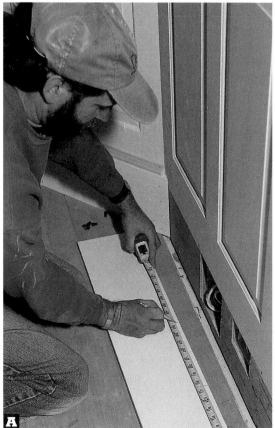

A

TRADE SECRET

In retrofit work, it's sometimes possible to locate an existing outlet box on the baseboard by painting the edge of the box with lipstick, and then pressing the back of the baseboard against the box. This leaves an outline of the box on the back of the baseboard. Make sure you clean up the edge of the electrical box, or you'll likely get lipstick on clean wood, complicating the finish process (and irking the electrician).

WHAT CAN GO WRONG

Don't attach a single piece of trim to both a wood floor and a masonry wall, as the differential movement between the dissimilar materials will loosen the connection over time or cause the wood to split.

B

C

D

drill a starter hole in one corner of the cutout **C**.

4. Insert the blade through the large starter hole and cut out the outlet opening with a jigsaw **D**.

5. Position the baseboard over the outlet and nail it in place **E**.

Wall heating registers are often taller than baseboard, creating an awkward trim detail. The easiest solution is to install the heat registers flush to the wall and then cut an open bevel on the end of the baseboard to create a flared effect. In this case, the long point of the open bevel should just touch the edge of the finish grille. The shoe molding should also have an open bevel on it, with the long point meeting the short point of the baseboard cut.

E

Another design solution is to install the heat registers a baseboard thickness away from the finished wall. In this case, the finish grille of the heat register laps over the square-cut ends of the baseboard, and the base cap wraps around the sides and top of the register. If one-piece baseboard is used, rip the top edge off a length of baseboard and use it to wrap the register, mitering it where it meets the baseboards and at the two outside corners.

Attaching trim to masonry Commonly, masonry is wrapped with wood baseboard when a brick chimney rises up through a corner of a room. In this case, I usually prebuild the corners—securing the outside miter separately— and then attach the two pieces as a single unit. Make sure that you attach the baseboard only to the floor.

Sometimes it's not possible to prebuild a large section (for example, along the length of an exposed brick wall). In that case, attach the baseboard only to the masonry. Frequently, it's possible to nail through masonry joints with standard finish nails. If not, sink in a couple of masonry anchors, and then screw the baseboard to the wall.

Countersink the screws so you can plug the heads. You'll be surprised how just a few screws hold baseboard in place, especially if you use a few daubs of construction adhesive on the back of the baseboard to help secure it. Shoe molding can be attached to the floor to help hold the baseboard in place.

Bending baseboard

Occasionally, you may have to bend baseboard around a curved wall. The easiest way to accomplish this is with multiple layers of thin plywood, with each layer individually bent to fit the curve. By building up several layers, you can produce

BASEBOARD MEETS HEAT: TWO REGISTER SOLUTIONS

Solution 1

The existing register is flat against the wall.

The base and shoe is cut at an angle for a "flared" effect.

Solution 2

Rip off the top portion of a single-piece base and miter it around the register.

Carry the cap molding around the register with a miter.

Register held out from wall

Bevel

a standard baseboard dimension. Then cover the exposed top edges of the plywood with base cap. For a natural wood finish, use an appropriate hardwood plywood for the final layer.

I prefer to use lauan plywood, which is cheaper and often more readily available than ¼-in. AC plywood. Take care, however, to select good lauan, as voids within the core will make the strip snap with only a little bending. Both fir and lauan plywood curve to smaller radii when bent across the face grain rather than parallel to it (see the chart on p. 80). Therefore, it is often easier to use several short sections cut across the 4-ft. dimension than it is to force a long run into place. Just be sure to stagger the joints from one layer to the next.

(see the chart on p. 80)

TRADE SECRET

When bending baseboard to fit a curved wall, I use a hardwood-veneered lauan for the outermost lamination—even for painted trim. Standard lauan face veneers have an open, porous surface that telegraphs easily through the painted surface.

Bending Radii for Dry Plywood or Dry Panel

Panel Thickness	Bent Across Grain	Bent Parallel to Grain
¼ in.	2 ft.	5 ft.
⅜ in.	3 ft.	8 ft.
½ in.	6 ft.	12 ft.
⅝ in.	8 ft.	16 ft.
¾ in.	12 ft.	20 ft.

Note: The radii shown are minimums; an occasional panel may develop localized fractures at these radii. (This chart was adapted from APA).

CLAMPING A CURVED BASE

Clamping blocks screwed into studs above a curved baseboard help secure the final layer of plywood while the glue sets up.

2 clamping block screwed to stud above baseboard

Finish floor

Drywall

Lauan temporary blocking (doubled and tripled for second and third layers, respectively)

Baseboard built up from multiple plywood layers

Construction adhesive between drywall and first baseboard strip

Screws hold first layers.

Stud

First lauan baseboard strip

Plate

Subfloor

For tight curves, you need to soak the plywood. To wet the plywood, stack wet towels on each strip. Use warm water and let the strips soak for several hours, rewetting the towels as necessary. Keep the area warm, especially when bending the piece into place. Wood fibers are elastic when warm but brittle when cold.

For a convex curve, you'll do things a little differently:

1. Begin at one end (for a concave curve, begin in the center) and screw the strip securely to a stud (don't set the screws too deep or they will pull through). As you wrap the strip around the curve, fasten it in a zigzag pattern to the studs and screw high and low.

2. For the next layer, reverse the pattern—going low, then high. Paint each layer with glue before applying the next layer. Wet plywood does not affect the overall strength of water-based glue (I use aliphatic resin—a standard yellow carpenter's glue), but the setting and drying times are significantly longer.

3. Finally, glue the finish layer, securing it in place with nails, not screws. Clamp it with a block on every stud. The nails prevent this layer from slipping around (see the illustration at left).

Stock cap and shoe moldings bend quite easily. Soak the molding in water if you have some particularly tight curves. A rabbet in the bottom edge of the molding helps keep the plywood edge hidden should the molding move during seasonal changes (see the illustration on the facing page).

Standard base caps can be used to cover the top edges of the lauan layers of a curved baseboard. If the width doesn't exactly match, the cap may need to be ripped down slightly. Run the base cap through a tablesaw, taking care to hold the back face firmly to the fence.

½ in.

¾ in.

1¹⁄₁₆ in.

1¹⁄₁₆ in.

Two layers of ³⁄₁₆-in. lauan (¼ in. nominal)

Three layers

³⁄₈ in.

⁹⁄₁₆ in.

TRADE SECRET

To fill nail holes, many professionals rely on an epoxy-based automotive filler, such as Bondo®. It sets up hard and won't shrink, but you have to mix it in small batches and work fast. Use a clean, sharp putty knife to scrape the filler flush with the surface and minimize sanding.

Finishing up

Before painting baseboard, caulk all of the small gaps. Gaps are especially conspicuous along the base cap and shoe moldings, which twist to conform to floors and walls at a rate different than the underlying baseboard. For painted trim, run a thin bead of a latex acrylic caulk along the top of the shoe molding, under the base cap, and along any open inside or outside corners. Wipe the joints down with a damp sponge to smooth out the caulk and push it into the gaps. Also, fill the nail holes with wood putty while you are still wearing your knee pads.

When filling nail holes, put a daub of wood putty on the end of a 1-in. putty knife, fill the hole, and use the knife to scrape as much putty as possible off the surface. After the putty has dried, sand lightly with 100-grit sandpaper before finish painting.

DESIGN
OPTIONS

◄ Wrapping baseboard around the end of a wall creates a classic column. The elaborate base cap here is made with three simple pieces: a 1x6 baseboard, a narrow (1¼-in. x ½-in.) lattice molding, and a traditional ogee base cap. The addition of the lattice molding creates a recessed channel that adds an extra dimension to the baseboard.

▲ The shoe molding doesn't always have to match the baseboard. Here, the choice of a stained hardwood shoe draws more attention to the parquet floor, while the simple white baseboard recedes into the wall.

▶ The tall ogee base cap on a relatively short 1x4 baseboard provides a strong visual base as it wraps around the bottom of a built-in window seat. The trim at the top of the window seat mirrors the window apron, unifying the space.

▲ Baseboard serves as a visual
foundation for not only the
walls but also a built-in
window seat. The baseboard
wraps the bottom of each
support for the window seat
and is carried around to support the hearth as well, tying
each architectural element
of the room together. Without
this unifying band, each part
would stand apart, appearing
more like a piece of furniture
placed in the room than an
integral part of the house.

◀ A traditional three-
piece baseboard wraps
the bottom of a frame-
less opening, provid-
ing an unbroken link
between dining room
and kitchen. The base-
board also provides
a foundation for the
built-in cupboards.

CROWN MOLDING

Nothing dresses up a room like crown molding does. Whether you install a brightly painted flat band or introduce fine shadow lines with a profiled molding, crown draws the eye upward and establishes a stylistic tone for the entire room.

Angled between the ceiling and the wall, crown molding inhabits a uniquely three-dimensional space. Although this three-dimensionality adds to the visual appeal of crown, it also makes it one of the most demanding pieces of trim to install. When the room turns a corner, the molding makes two turns— one along the ceiling and one along the wall, requiring compound cuts to join the angles. Plus, crown molding is subject to the shifting house movements acting on both planes, so it must be nailed securely to a flat, stable surface to keep the joints crisp and tight over time. ▶ ▶ ▶

SIMPLE CROWN PROFILES

Band Molding

In essence, band molding is upside-down baseboard; however, it is more noticeable because it isn't covered up by furniture. Although simple in design, it can be tough to install if the ceiling isn't flat or level. In that case, you can install the trim a bit lower down and cover the gap with a more flexible molding, such as scotia or quarter-round.

Bed Molding

While they are often not much more than 2 in. wide, bed moldings also have a spring angle—typically at 45°, 35°, or 32°. They are commonly used at the top of ornate head casings to fill in around coffered ceilings or encased beams. When used in conjunction with other moldings, they are also a popular choice for large, built-up cornices.

Cove Molding

Any molding with a hollowed-out curve is called cove molding. Large cove can be tough to join, because the long, sweeping inside curve can become a void if it is not cut precisely. Small cove is typically called scotia, and it is relatively more forgiving.

Ogee Molding

Standard ogee is most often what people mean when they say "crown molding."

Crown Basics

Crown molding can be any angled trim that fits between the ceiling and the wall, including ogee crown, cove, and bed moldings. These profiles can be used alone as single-piece moldings or combined to create various complexities of built-up crown.

Design considerations

In my opinion, traditional profiled crown works best in older homes with high, smooth plaster ceilings. The higher the ceiling, the larger the crown can be. If the ceiling is 10 ft. or higher, consider installing an ornate built-up cornice (see "Built-Up Crown Molding" on pp. 101–103). More contemporary homes with lower ceilings, textured surfaces, or patterned tile ceilings call for simple cove or band moldings made from flat stock.

Two design principles are at work here: contrast—ornate moldings accent smooth surfaces and smooth moldings accent textured surfaces—and proportion—large moldings can overpower a small space. Many houses have a standard ceiling height of around 8 ft. (give or take a few inches) and smooth drywall or plaster surfaces. In most of these cases, standard (3-in. to 4-in.) crown works well.

Spring angles

Crown molding always sits tilted between the wall and the ceiling. The angle of this tilt is called the spring angle, which is the angle at which the molding springs off the wall. Each size and style of crown molding has a different spring angle. Cove moldings often have a 45-degree spring angle, but the more common ogee-style crown moldings typically have a spring angle of 38 degrees.

Run

Ceiling

52°

38°

Drop

Spring angle

Wall

Crown molding has both a drop—the vertical height of the crown (measured on the wall)—and a run—the distance the crown projects out from the wall (measured on the ceiling). The angle at which it leaves the wall is called the spring angle.

Since crown molding has a complementary angle from the ceiling, it is often referred to by both angle numbers, such as 45/45-degree or 38/52-degree crown molding. Crown with a 38-degree spring angle is so common, in fact, that most manufacturers of compound-miter saws provide detents at the correct miter and bevel angles for cutting 38/52-degree crown.

Crown materials

Like other trim materials, crown materials fall into two categories: paint grade and stain grade (see "Paint Grade vs. Stain Grade" on p. 23). The most common paint-grade materials include finger-jointed pine, MDF, and poplar (for custom profiles). In recent years, MDF has become increasingly more available in a variety of sizes and profiles, and it has become my first choice for paint-grade work. It's relatively stable and able to resist the expansion and contraction of temperature and humidity changes.

When it is securely backed, the inside corners can be mitered and the scarf joints do not easily telegraph to the surface. This isn't necessarily the case with finger-jointed pine. Even when installed and primed well, I've been able to find finger joints after a heating season or two.

Stain-grade crown is typically run in hardwood, and because caulked joints aren't an option, it usually requires more cutting finesse. Instead of mitering the inside corners, the joints must be coped (see "Cope vs. Miter" below), and as you will soon discover, coping hardwood is especially challenging. You must be dead-on with your cuts, as there's no fudging a hardwood joint. In addition, a hand coping saw cuts slowly through denser material; most carpenters cut hardwood cope joints with a combination of power tools. However, there's no other choice than to cope hardwood crown, which will predictably move in any heating climate, turning tight miter joints into gaping gashes.

Cope vs. miter

Many production carpenters would argue that MDF is stable enough to allow you to miter the inside corners and not worry about them opening up when the wood shrinks. And it's true that it is far faster to miter rather than cope an inside corner, even if the miter must be recut a couple of times to precisely fit an out-of-square or out-of-plane corner. But even if the wood doesn't shrink, coping is far from a waste of time. In fact, I cope all inside crown joints, whether the crown is made from expensive hardwood or MDF. Regardless of the material, a cope joint is superior to a miter joint in masking the distortions of an out-of-level and out-of-square house.

Any house undoubtedly moves. The planes that exist when you install crown molding are

Compound-Miter Saws

COMPOUND-MITER SAWS come in two types. Both models tilt for the bevel and rotate for the miter. A fixed-base model has a cutting head that simply pivots from a fixed point in a manner similar to that of a standard compound-miter saw (see the left photo below). A sliding model has a cutting head that slides on a bearing-guided bar (or two) across the table in a manner similar to that of a radial-arm saw (see the center photo below). All sliding saws cut on the push, however, making them much safer to use than radial-arm saws. Dual compound-miter saws tilt in two directions, making it easier to cut bevels. Without this feature, you must flip the molding around, which can be quite a trick in a tight workspace.

A standard 10-in. power miter saw can miter sanitary base and other standard 2½-in.-high base stock held vertically against the fence (as shown in the right photo below). And while it can square-cut a 1x6, you'll need to upgrade to a 10-in. or a larger 12-in. miter saw in order to miter-cut a 1x6. For very tall stock, you'll need either a 12-in. compound-miter saw or a sliding compound-miter saw (which can miter-cut 5/4x10 stock or 1x12 stock). These large-capacity saws are more expensive, but they enable you to cut a wide variety of other trim stock, including shelving materials, large crown, floorboards, and jamb stock.

A compound-miter saw cuts both a miter and a bevel at the same time with the molding laid flat on the saw table. Most compound-miter saws have preset detents at the angle settings for common 38-degree crown. For crown with spring angles other than 38 degrees, you will need to calculate the angles when cutting it flat (easier said than done). Most saws include a list or chart of miter and bevel settings for a wide selection of crown. Although these saws are versatile (and expensive), you can't cut just any miter and bevel. If you have a 90-degree corner, for example, neither the miter nor the bevel is 45 degrees. Rather, the miter is 35 degrees and the bevel 30 degrees.

Standard fixed base.

Sliding compound-miter saw.

Beveling with a standard saw.

Each blade has a single row of jagged teeth oriented in one direction. Keep the teeth pointed toward the handle so you cut on the pullstroke. This keeps the blade in tension.

unlikely to be the same ones that emerge when a house settles during any given heating season. In my experience, a house never settles in permanently. Every house continually changes plane with seasonal fluctuations in temperature and humidity. Coped joints move like a knuckle, allowing these slight changes to occur without the joint opening up.

Other issues play into my decision to cope all crown joints. For one thing, I take a systematic approach to installing crown, which speeds up the job considerably. As I install the backer, I try to correct the plane, shimming out bulges and dips in both the ceiling and the wall. I also keep all cope angles in the same direction so that I don't have to continually reset my saw. Moreover, MDF, if used, is soft and uniform, making it exceptionally easy to cope. Finish cuts can be fine-tuned with a utility knife.

Prepping the Walls

Crown can be installed at the same time as other trim. Ideally, this is after the drywall has been taped and the ceiling has been primed but before the finish paint has been applied. In old houses,

where walls and ceilings are usually not smooth or flat, it's worth spending a little time mapping the area to find the low points and out-of-square corners.

Sagging ceilings and wavy walls

Since crown rests between the ceiling and the wall, it is subject to the imperfections in both planes. A sag in the ceiling or a wave in the wall creates a twist in the molding. Typically, ceilings are the worst. Most old houses have some kind of sag, usually a gentle curve toward the center of the room. One way to deal with it is to ignore it. Long lengths of crown are surprisingly flexible and often "wrap" around gentle bumps and shallow dips.

I always start a job by mapping the terrain with a builder's level and string to find the high and low spots. If the terrain is especially bumpy, I measure down the drop of the crown at the ends and snap a chalkline where the bottom edge of the crown should be. Then I cut the crown and tack it up, holding the edge to the chalkline.

If the ceiling sag is bad, I sometimes can't fit the crown on the chalkline, and if I force it, it throws off the corner joints. In this situation, there are three possible solutions. One is to scribe the top edge of the molding to the ceiling. To fit crown to an uneven ceiling, start by finding the low point, measure down the drop of the crown at that point, and snap a level line on the wall. Then cut the crown to length, tack it up along the line, and scribe the top edge. However, part of the visual appeal of most moldings is the parallel shadow lines created by the different ways light strikes the contours. So when scribing, don't bite too deeply into the top edge, or the nonparallel edge will be too easy to read. Generally, I don't scribe off more than a third of the top reveal.

TRADE SECRET

Most crown has a slightly rounded top edge, which provides a slight shadow line along the top. If you scribe the top edge of your molding to fit an uneven ceiling, make sure that you relieve the new edge with a block plane after cutting the scribe line. This preserves the shadow line and helps conceal the fix.

Skim-Coating

Another option is to bend the crown to lie flat along the uneven wall and ceiling, but this usually means that the corners don't align as they should. In that case, the angles must be scribed. To scribe the new angle, first cut the miter and reverse bevel as you would for a regular cope. This gets you close to the angle. Tack up the crown as close as possible to the meeting piece, with the long point of the reverse bevel against the meeting piece. Holding the scribe parallel to the ceiling plane, scribe a new angle. It's difficult to get a precise profile line with the scribe, so use this line mainly as a gauge for a new miter angle, which is then cut and coped as usual.

Probably the easiest fix is to let a good drywall taper or plasterer bail you out by skim-coating (or "floating") the ceiling and walls with plaster or joint compound to conceal any gaps after the crown has been installed. Instead of scribing the crown to an uneven ceiling, you can simply install it to a level line, leaving a visible gap between the molding and the ceiling except at the places where the crown meets the low spots. If you don't have solid backing behind the crown, you may need to slip shims into the gaps to provide a place for solid nailing along the molding edges. Cut the shims back, angling the knife behind the crown. These will later be covered along with the gaps by the skim coat of drywall mud, which is applied after the crown is in place.

Points of attachment

Don't expect to march up the ladder and begin firing nails. Finding nailing in the ceilings and walls can be much more difficult than you expect. Start by figuring out how the crown molding will be attached.

At the very least, plan to spend some time mapping the stud and joist layouts. In a new house, you can fly as soon as you know the nailing, and it's usually on even centers, so it's easy to map. This isn't necessarily so in an old house where stud and joist layouts can be on uneven intervals, and weak plaster and wavy drywall create soft spots that defy secure nailing. Also, nailing into stud and joist layouts means that the crown is secured along only the top and bottom edges—the thinnest and least stable portions of the molding. Inevitably, the edge will either split or the relatively small finish nails won't find purchase and will pull through the plaster or drywall. I have learned to avoid such aggravations by installing a rough backer first.

For standard crown, I typically make backers out of straight 2x materials ripped at a bevel to match the spring angle. Rather than cut the backer to completely fill the space behind the crown, I lay it out and cut it so that the top edge is ⅛ in. to ¼ in. shy of the back of the crown . This provides a gap behind the crown, allowing me to adjust the position, if necessary. The crown still firmly contacts the ceiling and wall at the edges, but it is pinned into the meaty belly with a stout finish nail.

To find the dimensions for ripping 2x4 backer, draw a section of the crown on a clean piece of plywood.

First, lay a framing square on the plywood to represent the wall and ceiling of the room, and then hold the end of scrap crown molding exactly as it will lie on the wall. Trace the line of the back side of the crown and the angle of the framing square . This gives you a precise layout from which to pull your numbers for ripping the backer, which can be read off the framing square .

PRO TIP

When installing straight backer material, leave an adjustment gap into which you can push the edges of the molding. You'll then conform to the ceilings and walls

Rip the backer at the bevel you've marked **D**. When complete, the backer should be under-sized by about ⅛ in. to ¼ in. from the back side of the crown **E**.

On at least two walls in every room, ceiling joists run parallel to the wall framing, so there may not be nailing in the ceiling. Some partition walls may have some cross blocking, which I try to pick up. But mostly I screw the backer into the studs and top plate, driving 3-in. screws at an angle into the top plate **F**. Don't be shy about riddling the rough backer with screws to hold

it in place. It doesn't have to look pretty; it just needs to be secure.

Backer isn't able to correct for all the dips in a ceiling or wall, though it does get most of them, and it helps hold the entire assembly of pieces more securely to the structure. Still, there's no way to avoid some gaps between the molding and the ceiling or wall. For paint-grade work, you can caulk the gap if it's less than ⅛ in. For wider gaps, or gaps around stain-grade crown, float drywall to fill the gap.

Installation Strategy

Before I actually start chopping up crown, I like to scope out the installation order, much in the same way that I do for baseboard.

First piece same as the last

To avoid having to cut a double cope (coped joints on both ends of the same piece of mold-ing) and to eliminate the time and fuss of resetting my saw for each cut, I set up all my cuts in the same direction. Usually, I start with the trim on the longest wall opposite the door, making one end coped and the other end butted square into the corner. Because I'm left-handed, I typically butt right, cope left. Find what suits you and stick to it. The direction is less important than consistency so that you don't have to constantly reset the angle on your saw.

Starter block

If you set up all your cuts in the same direction, the first piece of molding must be installed with a temporary block to fit against the coped end. This block consists of a scrap piece of 1-ft.-long crown, which is cut square to fit in the corner and temporarily screwed to the backer (see the top photo at right). I typically install this starter block, then measure and cut the first length, install that, and then work my way in one direction around the room. Nail the first piece of crown near the center toward the butt end only. This provides enough support to hold up the entire length of crown but leaves the coped end free so that you can remove the starter block and slip the last, full-length piece of crown in place.

Evaluate outside corners

If the room has an outside corner, it might make sense to start at that point. If you have more than one outside corner, consider cutting them all at once (for example, cut all of the right-hand miters and bevels at once, and then cut all of the left-hand miters and bevels). I still try to map out the cuts so that all of the compound cuts for the copes are angled in the same direction. If the legs of the outside corner are short (for example, at the top of a small bump-out in a room), you may need to temporarily tack up the coped leg of the

A starter block is temporarily screwed to the backer. Nail the first piece of crown that meets this block at the butt end only.

outside corner. This lets you later remove it to fit the last piece of crown that laps behind it.

Rooms with bump-outs often have a few very small pieces of crown. In this case, continue to cut all the copes in the same direction, but cut the compound angle and cope the piece before you cut it to length.

Measuring crown lengths

Because of the mud buildup in corners, it's often hard to get an exact reading by bending a tape measure into the corner. Even the most practiced carpenter can misjudge exactly where that bottom edge of the cope joint will land, especially when taking repeated measurements. Therefore, for most crown measurements I use pinch sticks, butting one end to the previously installed length and the other end to the wall. Pinch sticks are critical in tight, enclosed spaces, such as alcoves. Short lengths of molding aren't very flexible, so the length must be perfect.

On very long runs, it's not as critical to make a set of pinch sticks (I certainly don't take the time to make a set to measure just one long wall). Instead, I rely on a tape measure, aiming for a cut length that is 1/16 in. to 1/8 in. longer than the actual measurement. You can then bend this piece slightly to get it in place. If it's slightly long, it will snap into place and the points of the back cut will dig into the wall.

Cutting Crown

Crown molding can be especially challenging to cut because it already has one angle—the spring angle—built into it. However, if you always keep track of which edge is the bottom and which edge is the top and constantly picture how the molding will sit when it is nailed in place, you can usually puzzle through all the cuts.

As with all trim cuts, I try to group similar cuts together. That is, I first cut all the scarf joints, then all the outside miter joints, then all the inside corners. This strategy saves time with any trim. With crown molding, it's especially helpful because it helps you keep track of the three-dimensional orientation of the molding.

Scarf joints

Crown molding usually comes in 12-ft. lengths and rarely longer than 16-ft. lengths. If a wall is longer than the crown stock available, you'll need to splice, or scarf, two lengths together. I make all these scarf joints first (there usually aren't too many). In effect, I focus on manufacturing the longest lengths of molding first, and then look at the other types of cuts, tackling one type at a time. For scarf joints, I depend on two critical devices: a biscuit and a splint.

Biscuit A biscuit holds the two pieces of scarf joints in alignment.

1. Cut a 20-degree-angle bevel and a 20-degree-angle miter, or a 20-20 compound cut, on one end of the molding, then cut a corresponding 20-20 compound cut on the mating piece **A**.

A

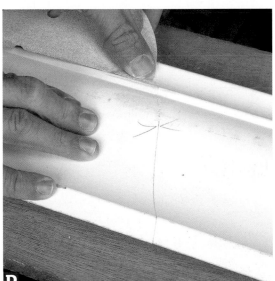

PROTIP

I use a standard 10-in. miter saw for cutting crown that is less than 4 in. wide. In fact, I prefer this saw because I only need to worry about the miter angle. By setting the molding on the saw at the spring angle, a single miter automatically cuts the bevel. The only drawback is that the saw has a limited depth of cut: Large molding doesn't fit in the saw at an angle. For that, you'll need a larger miter saw, or you'll need to cut molding flat with a compound-miter saw.

2. Lay the molding and the biscuit jointer flat on the same surface (usually on a workbench or the floor) and make biscuit slots in each piece. Elevate thinner moldings slightly by placing them on a piece of ⅛-in.-thick lauan. The slot should fall somewhere in the center thickness, not in the contoured face of the molding. The long point of the bevel holds the biscuit jointer away from the center area where the slot is cut. By setting the biscuit jointer to the maximum depth, you gain enough depth to fit a smaller #10 biscuit into the slot **B**.

Splint A biscuit guarantees alignment, but it doesn't hold the end grain together well. To fasten the two pieces more securely, make a thin wood splint.

1. Cut a strip of ¼-in.-thick lauan to act as a splint across the back. Keep in mind that if you use backer, you must cut the splint narrow enough and hold it near the bottom edge of the molding, so that it won't get in the way, or leave out the backer where the splint will fall.

2. Fasten this splint with plenty of glue and ½-in. staples in a standard T-50 staple gun **C**. The staples hold the strip in place until the glue cures.

3. After securing the splint to the scarf joint, you may need to smooth out the meeting edges with sandpaper **D**.

Interior Wood Glues

TITEBOND® IS SIMPLY a yellow glue colored brown so it won't show up on dark wood. However, I've never thought this to be a useful feature of glue, since all glue should be thoroughly wiped or sanded off before finishing, and joints should be airtight, rendering glue lines invisible. For most interior work, I use regular yellow carpenter's glue (center), which often has *aliphatic resin* on the label.

Yellow glue is stronger than ordinary white glue, and it's more heat resistant, so it doesn't melt as easily under the assault of a sander and instantly gum up the paper. When I'm working in high-humidity areas, such as a kitchen or bathroom, I typically use a Type II, or cross-linked PVA, glue (right). Although not exactly waterproof (meaning that it can't be used outdoors), it's a good choice when I'm using only one type of glue. While it cleans up with water, you'll need to work quickly with it, as it is noticeably tackier and has a shorter drying time than ordinary yellow glue. As a rule, if a wood glue can be cleaned up with water, it's for interior use; if solvents are needed, save it for exterior use.

Compound miters

The method I use to cut inside and outside corners depends on the type of saw. I prefer using a conventional miter saw and a simple jig that holds the crown at an angle, similar to the way in which it will be installed. When you set the saw for a simple miter, the orientation of the molding automatically provides the bevel angle. However, crown doesn't fit, unless you have a very large miter saw.

The alternative is to cut the crown flat with a sliding compound-miter saw. In general, sliding compound-miter saws are more versatile machines, but you must find the correct saw setting, which isn't necessarily obvious.

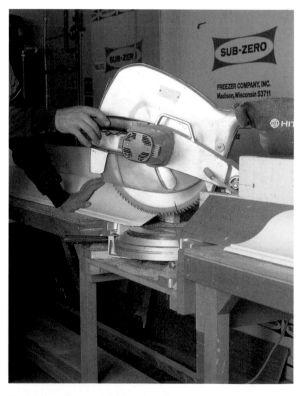

To help align molding at the correct angle in the saw, I make a simple jig with two strips of plywood screwed together at a right angle along the saw fence and table. I then apply a third strip of wood to hold the exact position for the top edge of the crown (the edge that's down on the saw table).

Cutting Crown Flat

WHEN CUTTING CROWN with a sliding compound-miter saw, the molding must lie flat on the saw table. To set the miter and bevel angles on the saw, use the settings in the chart at right, which are based on the spring angle of the molding. Before making the cut, keep track of the top edge of the molding. Depending on the type of cut you are making, either the top edge or the bottom edge lies against the fence. The photo sequences shown here demonstrate the correct orientation for each type of cut. (Note: With a dual compound-miter saw, you do not have to flip the molding around like this. Instead, simply tilt the cutting head in the opposite direction.)

Angle Settings for Sliding Compound-Miter Saw

Type of Crown (spring angle in degrees)	Miter (angle on table in degrees)	Bevel (tilt of blade in degrees)
30	27	38
35	30	35
38	31.5	34
40	33	33
45	35	30
52	38	26

COPED INSIDE CORNER

Left-hand piece: Top edge against fence.

Right-hand piece: Bottom edge against fence.

MITERED OUTSIDE CORNER

Left-hand piece: Bottom edge against fence.

Right-hand piece: Top edge against fence.

Get Corner Angles Right

Outside corners

Crown outside corners must be joined by compound miters. You also need good backer for outside corners. Any crown over 4 in. wide should have continuous backer behind the corner (the backer should also be mitered). For crown less than 4 in. wide, you can end the backer at the corner and simply rely on small finish nails to hold the miter closed, provided that it was cut accurately in the first place.

If an outside corner is square (use a framing square to check it) and you have a crisp corner (drywall corner bead, for example), you can just measure along the bottom edge and cut the molding at a 45-45 compound miter. To measure the length for an outside miter, hold the stock in place and mark where the bottom edge of the molding passes the outside corner. Remember that drywall corner bead pushes the corner out slightly, so you may have to back-plane the miter to get a tight fit (see the photo below).

If the wall corner is slightly out of square, an outside miter may need to be back-planed to fit tightly.

Plaster corners may be slightly rounded, making it difficult to measure the exact length along the crown's bottom edge. If the walls are reasonably square to one another (and only the very corner is rounded), here's how to fit it:

1. Mark the ceiling where the top edges of the molding meet. This lets you measure the length along the top edge to the long point of each miter cut. Position a length of crown along one side of the outside corner and draw a line where the molding meets the ceiling near the outside corner **A**.

2. Then position the opposing length of crown along the other side of the corner and mark the ceiling **B**. The intersection of the two ceiling lines represents the long point of a 45-45 compound miter on each length.

3. After cutting the miters, check the fit of the outside corner before nailing it in place **C**.

In an old house, the corner may be out of square, so the miter will not be a 45-45 compound cut. This situation requires a more elaborate method to find the exact miter angle (see "Bisecting an Angle" at right).

Inside corners

You can cut inside corners in two ways: with a cope or with a miter. As I mentioned earlier, I prefer to cope all crown molding. However, MDF materials can be joined with a compound miter, which is the fastest and simplest cut.

Inside miter To cut an inside miter, measure the length of the molding along the bottom edge. Remember that the long point of all inside miters will be on the bottom edge. Set up the molding exactly as you would for an outside miter but cut the opposite, or reverse, bevel.

For inside miters to fit well, the wall and ceiling planes must be nearly square and reasonably flat. Otherwise, the molding will twist and the inside miter won't fit tightly without a lot of fuss.

Coped joint A coped inside miter starts with a miter and a reverse bevel to expose the profile to be coped.

Bisecting an Angle

CARPENTER, BOATBUILDER, AND WRITER Jim Tolpin taught me a simple method of measuring the exact bevel setting for an out-of-square corner using a bevel board. The bevel board is nothing more than a piece of wood with some very carefully drawn angled lines ranging from 0 to 90 degrees. I made mine using a simple protractor and a very sharp pencil. To get the exact bevel angle for an out-of-square corner, start with two short scraps of wood that overlap at the corner.

1. Mark the long point of the angle on the underlapping piece **A**.
2. Mark the short point on the same piece **B**.
3. Find the angle on the marked piece with a bevel square. Then lay the bevel square on the bevel board and read the angle **C**.

PROTIP

Since the corners of a room tend to be slightly rounded with a heavy buildup of mud, I back-cut all the square ends.

1. If you're cutting with a standard miter saw, set the molding in the saw just as you would for an outside miter. However, rotate the table so that you cut the opposite, or reverse, bevel. This exposes the face of the crown, giving you the exact shape of the profile to cut with the coping saw **A**.

2. Mark the edge of the profile with the flat of a pencil lead, highlighting the contoured edge so that you can cut along the line with a coping saw.

3. Cut the profile with a coping saw **B**. I always back-cut slightly by tilting the coping saw past 90 degrees so that the meeting piece of molding can "pass by" cleanly **C**.

The coped piece should intersect only along the profile line. When cutting with a coping saw, I typically saw toward the curve from different directions so that I don't have to twist the saw and risk breaking the fragile edge of the profile **D**.

4. After cutting out the bulk of the material, smooth out the back cut with a rasp **E** until you have a smooth, sharp, feathered edge **F**.

5. To install the coped piece, predrill holes in the meaty portion of the crown's profile before nailing to avoid splitting the piece **G**.

Built-Up Crown Molding

So far, all of the techniques I have described in this chapter apply to single-piece crown moldings, ideally from 2½ in. to 4½ in. wide. Large rooms with high ceilings call for much larger moldings; at this size, they are commonly referred to as "cornice moldings." While it's possible to have large one-piece crown custom milled, a much more stable (and often less expensive) alternative is to build up large crown from several smaller profiles.

Simple Built-Up Crown

Built-up crown need not be complex—it can be as simple as a one-piece base and a stock ogee crown.

1. Snap a line on the wall that represents the bottom-most edge of the assembly, and then install a piece of standard colonial baseboard molding stock on that line. Install the base stock upside down, with the profiled cap hanging down, and screw through the middle of the wide, flat area of the molding with screws that are long enough to penetrate at least 1 in. into the studs or top wall plates **H**.

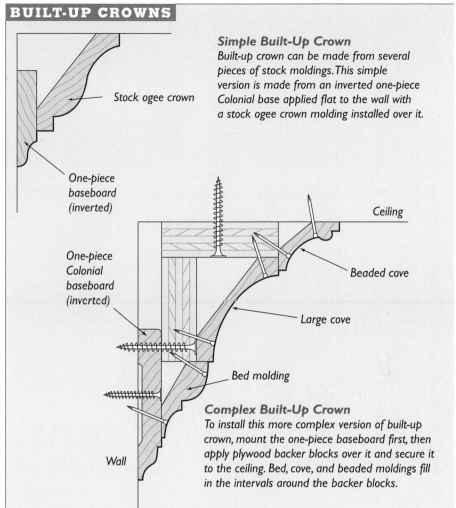

BUILT-UP CROWNS

Stock ogee crown

One-piece baseboard (inverted)

One-piece Colonial baseboard (inverted)

Wall

Ceiling

Beaded cove

Large cove

Bed molding

Simple Built-Up Crown
Built-up crown can be made from several pieces of stock moldings. This simple version is made from an inverted one-piece Colonial base applied flat to the wall with a stock ogee crown molding installed over it.

Complex Built-Up Crown
To install this more complex version of built-up crown, mount the one-piece baseboard first, then apply plywood backer blocks over it and secure it to the ceiling. Bed, cove, and beaded moldings fill in the intervals around the backer blocks.

2. Snap a line on the upside-down baseboard that represents the bottom edge of the crown molding. This reference line can be snapped before or after the base stock is installed. It's

PRO**TIP**

When wood is removed from one side of the board when milled, large crown or cove can cup and twist. A large cornice built from smaller components is more stable.

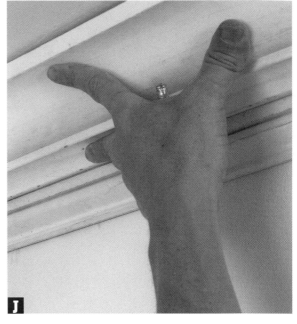

more important that the bottom edge of the crown align with the profiled edge of the base stock than with the ceiling. There may be bumps in the ceiling that show up along the top edge of the crown once it is installed, but the relationship of the crown edge and the profile baseboard will be most noticeable when the cornice is completed.

3. Check the fit of the crown molding with a scrap of crown molding. I typically use this to draw a reference line on the ceiling as well **I**.

4. Nail the crown on the base stock **J**. A small crown can be supported with nails along the bottom edge. Larger crown may require the addition of backing as described previously. Don't glue the individual moldings together. They should be free to move independently of each other to accommodate changes in temperature and humidity. However, you may want to use a bead of adhesive latex caulk, such as Phenoseal, to hold the crown molding to the ceiling.

Complex Cornice

A more complex variation on the same idea also uses standard base stock and standard crown moldings, with the addition of plywood backer blocks that help hold several pieces of molding in the right position. Standard moldings can be mixed and matched to create various cornice designs. Almost any molding, including bed, picture rail, screen bead, baseboard, and flat stock, will work. For example, dentils—a common feature of Federal-period crown—can be fashioned from 5/4 stock and inserted between the frieze (inverted base stock) and the crown (see the illustration on the facing page).

Depending on the cornice configuration, backer can be built from 1x and 2x material or from plywood for wider cornice moldings. The backer doesn't need to be continuous; it can be made of individual blocks spaced on 16-in. to 24-in. centers. Also, the backer doesn't need to wrap continuously around outside corners—two blocks on each side is sufficient. However, I prefer to build right-angled blocks for the inside corners to provide a stable base for coped joints.

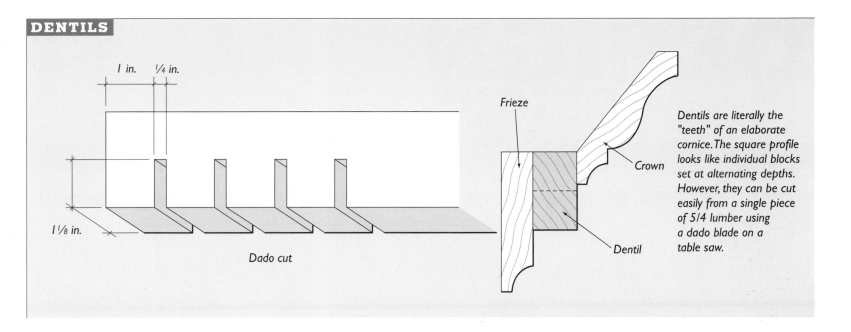

Dentils are literally the "teeth" of an elaborate cornice. The square profile looks like individual blocks set at alternating depths. However, they can be cut easily from a single piece of 5/4 lumber using a dado blade on a table saw.

I in.   ¼ in.

I ⅛ in.

Dado cut

Frieze

Crown

Dentil

1. For a complex cornice, the frieze is installed the same way it is for a simple built-up crown. The plywood backer blocks (which can be fashioned in advance from scrap plywood) are then screwed to the base stock **A** (on facing page). It works best if the backer blocks are attached only to the base stock, and the ceiling side is allowed to "float" **B**. This will accommodate any fluctuations in the ceiling.

2. After the backer blocks are in place, the subsequent moldings can be installed one layer at a time, starting from the bottom **C**.

When multiple pieces of molding are running parallel to each other, as they do in a complex buildup like this, remember to check your fit as you screw in each backer block. Snap reference lines for each run and check your fit using a scrap block of each molding type to be sure that the reveals are consistent at every step.

DESIGN
OPTIONS

▲ Crown doesn't have to wrap around every architectural element. The elegant crown in this classic colonial interior dies into the corner columns (the structural posts of a historic timber-frame house). The effect draws less attention to the structure than if the crown wrapped around the head like a column capital.

▲ This wide crown, which appears to be a single piece, is actually made from two moldings. The secret to joining the two moldings is the backing behind it.

▶ Deep-cut dentils in this crown create strong, rhythmical shadows that draw quiet attention to the trim without detracting from artwork.

▶ This Greek Revival crown features a dentil molding. No matter how complex the crown, it can still wrap around the angles of a room, as it does here, wrapping around the interior of an angled bay window.

WAINSCOTING

Traditionally, the term *wainscoting* has referred to any kind of wood wall paneling, though today it usually means paneling over the lower portion of a wall. Wainscoting was a common interior feature in American homes from the mid-1800s into the 20th century. Chair rail, which caps most wainscoting, once served a practical as well as a decorative purpose, protecting the wall from chairs set up against it. For Romantic- and Victorian-era homes, wainscoting is a period detail, but it adds traditional warmth and elegance to a contemporary house design, too.

First, we'll take a step-by-step look at the simplest wainscoting method, which uses vertical tongue-and-groove boards. Vertical board paneling is simple, economical, and quick to install, so it is the type that I install most often. Then I'll introduce a modified frame-and-panel system. Generally, such systems require more joinery, but the method shown here is much simpler, and it gives a good approximation of true raised panels. ▶ ▶ ▶

1 Designing Wainscoting
p. 108

2 Installing Backer
p. 111

3 Installing Tongue-and-Groove Wainscoting
p. 116

4 Installing Modified Frame-and-Panel Wainscoting
p. 119

5 Installing Chair Rail
p. 121

Designing Wainscoting

Because it covers such a substantial portion of the wall, wainscoting taxes the limits of wood's dimensional stability. Over a large area, the cumulative movement of many boards joined together can lead to substantial problems with cracked boards and open joints. Thus, any wainscoting design must account for the inevitable movement of wood that occurs with changes in humidity and temperature.

The simplest traditional method uses many relatively narrow tongue-and-groove boards. Each board is nailed along the tongue edge so that the groove edge is free to move. As the boards expand and contract, the groove slips over the tongue, and the overall movement of wood across the entire wall goes undetected. The other traditional approach uses molded, solid-wood panels that essentially float in a frame fixed to the wall.

Tongue-and-groove wainscoting

Also known as vertical-board wainscoting, tongue-and-groove wainscoting looks best in simpler house styles. It works well with country and colonial design schemes. With a simple, square-band chair rail, it can also fit in contemporary schemes designed to accentuate clean vertical and horizontal lines.

Tongue-and-groove wainscoting comes as individual boards sold in random widths, in standard widths from 2½ in. to 5 in., and in thicknesses ranging from ⅜ in. to ¾ in. Most home centers sell shrink-wrapped bundles of the thinner ⅜-in.-thick material in precut lengths from 3 ft. to 4 ft. Lumberyards often sell wainscoting in various thicknesses by the linear foot.

Although just about any tongue-and-groove boarding can be used for wainscoting, material sold expressly for this purpose typically has

WAINSCOTING BOARD PROFILES

Bead Board

3 in.

⅜ in.

V-groove

4½ in.

¾ in

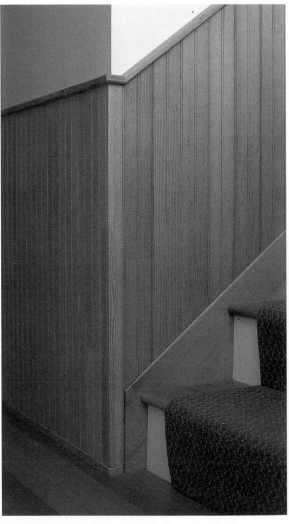

Bead-board wainscoting is the simplest to install and still adds an elegant touch to a room.

a milled profile—either a simple beveled edge, called V-groove, or a beaded edge, called bead board (see the illustration on the facing page). Wider widths often have an extra V or bead milled into the face as well. Some traditional-minded carpenters consider only bead board to be true wainscoting material and use V-groove as a finish ceiling board (common for porch ceilings). Combination material with a V-groove on one side and bead on the other is also available, though I have only seen it in ¾-in. thickness.

Frame-and-panel wainscoting

Frame-and-panel wainscoting seems most at home in the more elaborate interiors of Victorian and Queen Anne–style houses. True raised panels deal with the problems of cumulative wood movement as well as any woodworking method can. Yet, as ingenious and effective as this approach is, it is exceptionally difficult and time-consuming to execute well. I put raised panels right up there next to dovetails as one of the most challenging woodworking maneuvers.

It's possible to reproduce the look of frame-and-panel wainscoting with modern materials and simplified joinery. Sheet goods, such as plywood and MDF, are stable enough to allow you to reproduce traditional details using simple methods. The result may not be true frame-and-panel construction, but it will look elegant nevertheless (see the photo at right). And more important, with a minimal investment in time and expertise, the paneling will remain beautiful for as long as the house stands.

True raised-panel wainscoting.

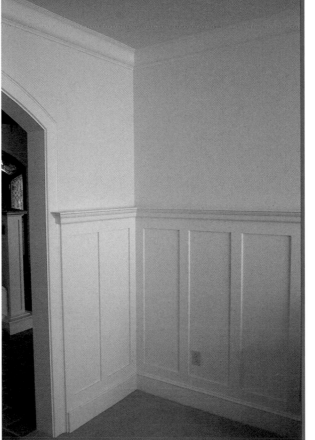

Modified frame-and-panel wainscoting with recessed panels.

Tall wainscoting, applied to just one wall, requires minimal work but provides a distinctive interior touch.

Planning your installation

Wainscoting varies in height, but as a general rule, it covers the lower third of a wall. So, for a typical 8-ft.-high ceiling, aim for wainscoting between 30 in. and 36 in. tall. I try to align the top rail with other features in the room. Countertops are typically 36 in. tall, bars are often 42 in. tall, and desks and tables are typically 30 in. tall. All of these features make acceptable wainscoting heights (including chair rail). In rooms with tall ceilings, wainscoting even looks good at 60 in. or taller.

Similarly, the base of wainscoting looks best when it matches the height of other baseboard in the house. I generally try to echo other baseboard heights when they can be seen prominently through doorways or around corners. But, like all design rules, this one can always be broken, as long as you do so deliberately.

The top rail, or chair rail, is often the most prominent feature of wainscoting. Choose a pro-

file for the top rail that matches, or in some way conforms to, the existing trim. If window and door casing is flat and plain, I aim for a simple square-edged band. More elaborate profiled trim calls for a built-up rail fashioned from several pieces of profiled molding.

With a frame-and-panel system, the rectangle becomes the primary design element, so you want to pay attention to the alignment, proportion, and orientation of these defining rectangles. I match the rail width to the casing width, so that the vertical band of the casing visually matches the stiles on the wainscoting (see the bottom photo on the facing page). In general, panels should be proportioned to match, or echo, other architectural elements, such as window sashes, door panels, or built-in cabinets. However, this proportional unit provides only a starting point, as it's often necessary to alter the width of panels in order to evenly divide wall areas.

The panel sizes of wainscoting should be planned carefully so they evenly divide wall areas.

As with all interior trim, a great deal of the design focuses on the details, such as the way the chair rail intersects with the door and window trim. These details can have a considerable impact on how long the job will take, depending on how simple or elaborate they are.

Installing Backer

All wainscoting needs solid backer in the walls for nailing. In new construction, many carpenters install blocking between the studs—usually three rows of 2x4 blocking installed "on the flat" near the wainscoting's top, bottom, and center. However, even in new construction, I prefer to install plywood backer over the studs, which provides continuous nailing for individual boards and reduces air leakage (see the photo on p. 112).

The many cracks between individual boards in both vertical-board and frame-and-panel

The stiles of this frame-and-panel wainscoting mirror the width of the door casing.

Using the Golden Mean

THE GOLDEN MEAN—A rectangular proportion of five to eight—is a useful design rule that is used often in construction. When I'm planning frame-and-panel wainscoting, and windows and casing aren't defining factors, I use the golden mean to establish the heights and widths of the grid. To preserve this proportion, the panels of tall wainscoting often run vertically.

Step 1: Draw a square the desired width of the rectangle.
Step 2: Bisect the baseline (point A) and extend a compass from A to the opposite corner (point B).
Step 3: Swing an arc from B to the baseline of the rectangle (point C), which is the length of the Golden Rectangle.

Modified frame-and-panel wainscoting begins with continuous plywood backer in place of drywall on the lower portion of the wall.

wainscoting create potential places from which air can leak to exterior walls. Unless you make an extra effort to keep the walls tight, these air leaks can allow warm air to escape and, in cold climates, create moisture problems inside the walls. The best way to avoid this problem is to replace the drywall behind the wainscoting with plywood, and then seal the top gap between the plywood and the drywall with expanding foam. If you opt to strip out the drywall to install horizontal nailers, seal the gaps with foam above and below each nailer on all exterior walls (see the illustration below).

Retrofitting a nailing base, or backer, in existing construction requires considerably more work. The best alternative—and one that provides continuous and stable nailing—is to remove the drywall or plaster and lath entirely

TRADE SECRET

The traditional way to provide nailing for wainscoting is to install 2x blocking between the framing. However, I prefer to install ½-in. or ⅝-in. plywood in place of drywall on the lower portion of the wall. This provides a more solid, continuous nail base.

WAINSCOTING BACKER

Nosing

Scotia

Board wainscoting

Let-in backer strips

Existing baseboard

Shoe moldings

Continuous plywood backer

Nosing

Scotia

Rail

Frame-and-panel wainscoting

Stile

Plywood shim for baseboard

Rail

New baseboard

behind the wainscoting and replace it with plywood.

The most economical alternative, though, is to cut out the drywall in strips and let in horizontal nailers.

1. Establish a level line for the top of the wainscoting. I snap a chalkline around the room, usually with blue chalk, which is water-soluble and can be washed off if the walls won't be repainted. This line represents the top edge of the chair rail that caps the wainscoting.

2. Below this top line, I lay out the locations for the nailing strips. The upper nailer should be just below the top line to provide nailing for the chair rail and the top end of the wainscoting. When I am working off an existing baseboard, I position the lower nailing strip a couple of inches above the baseboard. The nailer needs to support only the lower end of the wainscoting. However, if I am applying a new baseboard over the wainscoting, I want the lower nailing strip to provide backer for it as well.

All of these lines can be quickly established around the room with a layout stick. This is simply a narrow board that helps mark the height of chair rail and backer strips. Using a story pole saves time, since I only have to pull out my tape measure once to mark the stick. Hold the bottom end of a story pole on the floor (or the top edge of an existing baseboard) to transfer consistent heights **A**. I use a story pole to mark both sides of each corner, window, and door, and then I snap a chalkline to establish layout lines **B** and **C**.

Lasers for Interior Layout

ALTHOUGH IT MAY SEEM very high-tech, lasers are now widely used in measuring instruments, especially levels. Laser levels generate a visible laser beam with an electronic laser diode. The beam is too dim to see well in bright sunlight, but it shows up brightly indoors.

Contrary to the advertisements, however, these tools do not project a solid red line through space.

The basic "point-and-shoot" laser levels produce a small red dot where the laser beam hits the wall. Rotary instruments spin the laser beam and display a distinct line on the wall. By setting the instrument on a tripod and adjusting it for level, you can project a level line around the room to help you level cabinets, countertops, wainscoting, and chair rails.

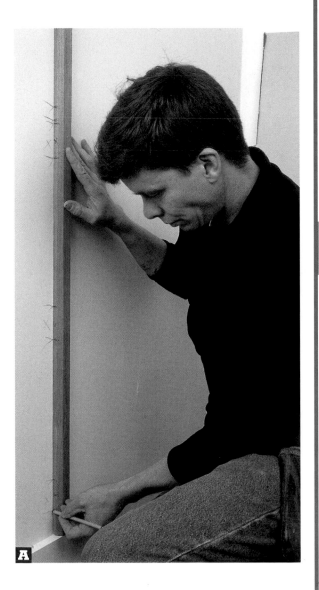

A

PROTIP

Red chalk is indelible and should be used only where it can be covered up. Blue chalk can be washed off.

3. Removing the old wall covering is often the most laborious part of retrofitting wainscoting. Cut through the drywall with a utility knife or cutout tool. I prefer to use a drywall cutout tool, such as Roto Zip®, because it is fast. To make clean up easier, be sure to hold a vacuum near the bit to capture a lot of the dust . Without this tool, you must cut along the layout lines with a utility knife, scoring the lines several times in order to cut completely through the old surface.

4. Pry out strips of the finish wall. To remove plaster, chip out the plaster with the claw end of a hammer and remove the wood lath strips. Be sure to pull out all the old nails from the edge of the studs so that you have a clean face on which to attach the horizontal nailers.

5. Determine the thickness of the nailing strips.

6. Screw in horizontal nailing strips **E**.

7. Secure the drywall above and below each strip along each stud, since many of the fasteners holding the drywall may have been removed.

Backer Thickness

THE THICKNESS OF THE BACKER depends on the thickness of the original wall surface. When installing continuous plywood backer, try to match the thickness of the wall covering (drywall or plaster), so that the wainscoting is applied to the same plane and projects forward. For let-in strip backer, I aim for backer that's slightly thicker than the wall, allowing the applied wainscoting to bridge any imperfections in the surface. This means that there will be a small gap between the back side of the wainscoting and the old wall, which will be covered at the top by the chair rail. For example, I use 5/4 material for let-in backer in walls covered by plaster and lath. For walls covered with ⅝-in. drywall, I use ¾-in.-thick (1x) nailers, and for ½-in. drywall, I use strips of ⅝-in.-thick plywood. All of these provide a nailing surface that sticks out slightly from the original wall.

When determining the thickness of the backer, check the thickness of existing baseboard and window and door casings. There may not be room to provide ample clearance for wainscoting and also preserve a nice reveal along the baseboard or window and door casings. In this case, you want to have at least a ⅛-in. reveal showing along the edge of the trim. If you're installing new trim, consider using 5/4 casing and perhaps shimming out the baseboard, so that these pieces of trim project well out from the surface of the wainscoting.

Use screws to secure backer strips in each stud. Also, secure the drywall above and below the backer strip.

Installing Tongue-and-Groove Wainscoting

If you haven't already done this when laying out the backer, start a wainscoting installation by snapping a level chalkline on the wall to indicate the height of the boards. If the floor is reasonably level, all of the boards can be cut to length ahead of time.

The boards should be installed plumb, but if they butt tight to the top edge of an existing baseboard, you may have to cut a slight angle on the bottom end of each one to create a tight fit with an out-of-level baseboard. In this case, you may have to cut each board one at a time, checking the fit as you go. If you do cut an angle on the bottom of each wainscoting board, be aware that the tops won't line up and will instead leave a serrated edge. However, the molding below the chair rail can cover this edge.

Base first

If the wainscoting will butt into a baseboard, make sure that the baseboard is installed first (see pp. 60–83 for information on installing baseboard). I like to have a ⅛-in. to ¼-in. reveal where the wainscoting meets the baseboard (depending on the thicknesses of the baseboard and the wainscoting). You can shim out the baseboard so that the wainscoting has an edge on which to sit.

If wainscoting runs all the way to the floor, cut a short piece of ¼-in.-thick plywood or lauan to put on the floor as a temporary spacer to make each board sit off the floor. This gap will later be covered by shoe molding or overlaying baseboard. If the boards butt tight to the top edge of the baseboard, provide a similar gap at the top, just below the chair rail. This makes the boards easier to install and leaves room for them to swell a little in the future, so that they don't buckle or split. The gap at the top will later be covered by cove molding (or a similar detail) running below the chair rail.

Board layout

I plan the layout so that the wainscoting begins with full widths around windows and doors. I leave partial widths to fall at inside corners, where they will be least conspicuous. If there are any outside corners in the room, I start there and work toward the inside corners.

Whenever wainscoting turns a corner—outside or inside—the boards must be flipped end for end, so that you always lead with a tongue. Wainscoting boards can simply butt door and window casing, but an intersecting chair rail should be notched to overlap the casing. Windows with a stool-and-apron design also require extra work. Both of these details are described in "Wainscoting Meets Window Stool" on p. 125.

Outside corners

For paint-grade work, outside corners can be butted edge to edge. I rip the grooves off two boards (also removing the beveled edge, if there is one) and plane the saw marks off to make a crisp edge. I then test-fit before gluing and nailing the corner closed with 4d (for ⅜-in. material) or 6d (for ¾-in. material) finish nails. I find it works best to nail the two pieces together at the corner, then attach the assembled corner unit to the wall, sinking the nail in a V-groove or near a bead.

For stain-grade work, it's best to miter the corner.

1. Start by ripping a 45-degree angle along the groove edge of two boards **A**.

2. Since it can be difficult to prenail a mitered corner, as you would if you were butting the corner, hold the two boards on the corner as close as possible to plumb **B**.

3. Tack one board to the wall **C**.

4. Apply glue to the corner and tack the second board in place **D**.

5. With the two boards secured, it's easier to push the corner closed and nail it tight **E**.

PRO TIP

For paint-grade work, outside corners can be butted edge to edge, but for stain-grade work, it's better to miter the corner.

Keep a short level handy
when you're installing
wainscoting, occasionally
checking that the boards
are plumb.

WHAT CAN GO WRONG

If a floor sags, you
don't want to mirror the
sag on the wall. In that
case, establish a level
line on the wall, snap a
chalkline, and then use
that as your benchmark
instead of the floor. Make
up for the sag in the
baseboard. If a floor has
a gentle slope, however,
it may be desirable to
mimic the slope in the
wainscoting so that you
end up with parallel
horizontal lines. This is
a judgment call that I
often need to make in
old houses.

PRO TIP

When working into a
corner, keep a Surform®
tool handy to level off
extra drywall compound.

Nailing straight runs

When there are no outside corners, I start at an
inside corner and face-nail the first board with
a single row of nails down the center of the
board. For each successive tongue-and-groove
board, nail only one edge (the tongue side) of the
board. Leave the other free to move—the floating groove slips over the stationary tongue—as
the boards expand and contract with changes in
temperature and humidity. Secure ⅜-in.-thick
boards with 4d finish nails; use 6d or 8d finish
nails for thicker material. I check for plumb as I
go (see the photo above). To adjust out-of-plumb
boards, push the gap between them slightly more
open at one end and slightly tighter at the other
end. If you have a board with an extreme bow,
don't force it over; instead, throw that board in
the scrap pile or cut it up for floor blocks.

When nailing, angle the nail toward the panel.
If you drive a nail straight in, it's likely to split the
fragile tongue. This is certainly one place where
I prefer to use a pneumatic nailer. Just make sure
that the nail sets all the way. Sometimes the nailer's

SAFETY FIRST

Air nailers are aptly called guns.
They fire a nail at a speed that can
seriously injure or even kill you.
Always stay out of the line of fire and
watch where your hands are. If you're
working with a helper, make sure he
or she is out of the way, too.

rubber tip gets in the way when nailing into a
corner at the tongue, leaving the head of the nail
high. In that case, set the nail by hand.

Inside corners

Inside corners butt tongue to groove. That is, the
tongue side of one board bolts into the corner,
and the groove side for the next run butts into
this same corner. Most of the time, however,
you'll have to rip the last board to width, so make
sure that you rip off the tongue, leaving the
groove for the next to last board to slip over
(as shown in photo C on the facing page).

V-groove and bead board look best when
identical-width boards face each other in the
corner. Therefore, if I rip the last board of a run
to width, I also rip the first board of the next run
to an identical width so that the adjacent corner
boards are mirror images of one another.

1. Measure the distance on the wall for the last
board in a run **A**. Transfer this distance to the
board **B**.

2. On the last board, rip the board to width,
cutting off the tongue side **C**. When ripping
the facing board, make sure you rip off the
groove and leave the tongue to continue the
next run.

3. If the walls are out of plumb, you can make up the difference by planing the last board to fit. Plane the last board of the run to a slight angle so it fits between the plumb boards and the out-of-plumb corner **D**. And when you turn the corner, start the next run as plumb as possible by cutting the meeting board at the same angle **E**.

Installing Modified Frame-and-Panel Wainscoting

If you have the time, expertise, and equipment, you can build true frame-and-panel wainscoting that will give a room the look of fine cabinetry. That project is beyond the scope of this book. For the same look at considerably less trouble and expense, you can build a modified frame-and-panel wainscoting system using sheet goods and simple joinery.

Construction details

I use a frame of 1x4 rails and stiles that I fix to a plywood, MDO, or MDF backer. The backer, which I usually refer to as the "ground" in this application, holds the 1x4 frame in place and remains exposed to simulate recessed panels (see the photo at right). For the look of raised panels, secondary MDF rectangles can be screwed to the ground between the grids created by the frame.

This system works best for painted wainscoting. If you want a natural wood finish, use high-quality veneer plywood as the ground and hardwood rails and stiles. I don't recommend screwing solid-wood fill panels to plywood unless they're narrow—no wider than 8 in. to 10 in.—and secured with a single center row of screws (countersunk and plugged). Otherwise, the panels are likely to split.

Install the ground directly to the wall studs in place of the typical drywall or plaster wall covering. Lightly tack each panel in place with a few 4d finish nails, then make layout marks on the plywood that describe where the rails and overlay panels will go. Permanently secure the ground with 2-in. wood screws, hiding the

Plywood backer serves as the surface for a recessed panel over which rails and stiles are applied.

screw heads below the rails (and overlay panels, if there are any) wherever possible.

I like to use clear poplar for the frame because it takes paint well, is relatively stable, and is often less expensive than clear pine. Typically, I install a 1x4 rail along the top, a 1x6 or 1x8 baseboard along the bottom, and 1x4 uprights in between. As always, select dry material to avoid cupping and warping, and prime the back side of the rail stock before cutting it to length and securing it to the ground.

Secure the rails with 1⅝-in. wood screws, countersinking the holes below the surface. Lay out the screws in a single line running down the middle of each rail, which allows the rails to move a little as they shrink and swell. In addition to screws, install biscuits at the ends of stiles where they intersect with the top and bottom horizontal boards. This helps align the surface of the boards and provides a tight joint that's less likely to crack the paint. I join the plates as I install the frame.

Countersink Nails

USE A NAIL SET, OR NAIL PUNCH, to countersink the head of a finish nail below the surface of woodwork. These typically come in sizes ranging from 1⁄16 in. to 5⁄32 in. for use with different size nails. I usually carry just two nail sets: 1⁄16 in. (often specified as 2⁄32 in.) for most finish nails and 1⁄8 in. for larger finish nails. For the occasional brad, I do have a 1⁄32-in. nail set in my toolbox, but I prefer to use a

brad setter rather than a hammer and nail set. When using nail sets, always wear safety glasses.

Prebuilt wainscoting panels

Although I typically build wainscoting panels in place, it's also possible to prebuild them in full-length sheets that can be attached to the wall studs in one piece. The panels can then be built in the shop under controlled conditions. On site, the panels are leveled and screwed to the framing to quickly finish a large wall area at one time.

1. Level the prebuilt panel **A**.

2. Screw securely to each stud **B**.

3. Apply drywall above the panel **C**.

Installing Chair Rail

Chair rail, which caps wainscoting, can be its own detail. In rooms broken up by a lot of windows, chair rail can provide plenty of extra interior detail where full wainscoting would be overkill. By itself, chair rail produces an immediate and powerful effect of dividing the wall height into unequal portions. Painting the two portions in different, complementary colors can enhance the effect.

When used in conjunction with wainscoting, chair rail should include a small finish trim below to hide the expansion gap, which is particularly important when wainscoting fits tightly to the baseboard. Although there are a number of possible chair rail configurations (see the illustration on p. 122), I typically cut a simple chair rail from 5/4 stock, ripping it to 1½ in. wide and rounding over the outside edge with a ¾-in. roundover bit (as shown in the bottom photo at right).

When I'm working with stain-grade chair rail, I usually nail it in place with stout 10d to 12d finish nails, angling them from the top down

If possible, rout the edges before ripping chair rail. When necessary, brace narrow stock against blocks clamped to a benchtop, as shown.

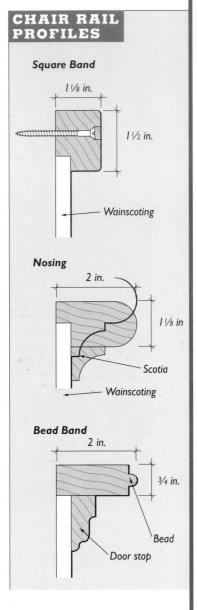

Square Band

1 1/8 in.

1 1/2 in.

Wainscoting

Nosing

2 in.

1 1/8 in

Scotia

Wainscoting

Bead Band

2 in.

3/4 in.

Bead

Door stop

The inside corners of rounded chair rail should be coped.

A scarf joint is used to join lengths of trim.

toward each stud in the wall. Predrill for these nails, then set the nail heads. A finish nail is easier to hide than a screw and plug.

As with other horizontal trim, such as baseboard and crown, the outside corners should be mitered and the inside corners coped. Similarly, linear runs of both the chair rail and the underlying scotia (a concave molding commonly used for horizontal transitions) should be joined by a scarf joint.

Scribing chair rail

Most of the time, chair rail must be scribed to the fluctuating surface of the wall. Besides uneven wall surfaces, outside corners usually have a buildup of mud near the corner bead, so they also require scribing. The problem is that scribing the rail can throw it out of parallel with the face of the wainscoting, so a miter at the outside corner may not be a perfect 45-degree angle. I approach the task this way:

1. Cut the rail on one side of the corner to length with a 45-degree miter on the end **A**.

2. Holding the rail on the top of the wainscoting, scribe the back edge of the rail to match the wall. Plane the rail to the line with a block plane **B**.

3. Predrill for a 10d finish nail and tack the scribed rail in place, nailing at an angle into a stud **C**.

4. Hold the next rail to the wall, pushing it hard to the outside corner and parallel to the face of the wainscoting. Mark the matching miter angle, tracing underneath the second rail and against the first rail **D**.

5. After cutting the scribed angle, scribe the rail to the wall, planing the back edge of the chair rail until it fits tightly **E**.

6. Nail the miter closed with opposing finish nails. If nailing by hand, be sure to predrill first **F**. Depending on how much is planed off the scribed edge, the outside corner may have to be fine-tuned with a block plane **G**.

7. Finish up the chair rail by installing trim molding **H**.

Caulk for Paint-Grade Trim

The intersections of different kinds of trim require planning and careful joinery.

A chair rail ends gracefully as it overlaps the door casing. Note the scotia ends at the edge of the casing.

Finishing details

The details at windows and doors take the most time and attention. The wainscoting can simply butt the casing (see the top photo above). The chair rail, however, should be notched so it overlaps, and the scotia below should butt the casing (see the bottom photo above). If the casing has a bead or a back band, notch the casing as well as the chair rail.

Around square-edged casings, you can simply notch the rail so that it overlaps the same distance as the thickness of the rail. However, when the casing has a back band or a beaded edge, you also need to notch the casing—in effect, weaving the joint together. Here's how:

1. Measure the dimensions of the notch by holding the rail on the wainscoting and marking the edges with a sharp pencil **A**.

2. Cut the notch in the casing. Here, carpenter Craig Tougas uses a Japanese pull saw, keeping it square to the edge of the casing by resting it on a block of wood **B**.

3. Once the sides have been cut, finish off the notch in the casing with a chisel **C**. Test-fit the notch by holding the rail in place. Mark the depth of the casing on the end grain of the rail.

4. Notch the rail with the same pull saw, using a rasp to smooth the edges to a crisp, square cut **D**.

5. When finished, check the final fit **E**.

Stools and aprons on windows require even more work. If the window is already trimmed, pull off the apron and replace it with a rabbeted apron. If the window hasn't been trimmed, use a scrap of casing stock to measure the distance from the jamb (including the reveal) to the outside edge of the casing, mark the wall, and run the wainscoting to that line. If it doesn't break on a full-width piece at the outside casing line, notch the wainscoting underneath the window. The notch then comes in under the stool or under the apron, depending on how you handle the apron.

Install the stool after the wainscoting is in place, so that the horns overlap the wainscoting, as shown. I've seen many carpenters cut a wide stool, then install the apron on top of the wainscoting. But I prefer to bring in the notch under a rabbet on the apron. This way, all of the window stools in the house are the same width, and all of the window trim—casings and aprons—lie on the same plane.

A

B

C

D

E

Casing

Chair rail

Notch stool to allow wainscoting to pass by.

Window stool

Rabbeted apron

Wainscoting

WAINSCOTING MEETS WINDOW STOOL

Casing

Chair rail

Window stool

Rabbeted apron

Wainscoting

Notch wainscoting board around stool and apron.

DESIGN
OPTIONS

▼ Wainscoting can run horizontally, as well. Here, battens made from thin, narrow lattice molding cover the horizontal joints between boards, adding a mildly rustic touch to a cabinlike interior.

▲ Wainscoting doesn't always have to extend to chair-rail height. Tall, vertical tongue-and-groove wainscoting (and matching ceiling) is a perfect choice for this country kitchen, where it extends above countertop height and provides a scrubbable backing to sink and stove.

◀ This modified frame-and-panel wainscot is made with plywood backer overlaid with 1x6 rails and stiles, then each recessed panel is framed with an ogee basecap. Baseboard and chair rail complete the composition.

▲ Besides its traditional application, wainscoting can also be used to provide interesting details in bathrooms.

BASIC BOOKSHELVES

From simple wall brackets that hold up plain boards to elaborate pieces of furniture, bookshelves come in a wide variety of designs. In this chapter, I'll describe my simple, adaptable method of building adjustable shelves with hardwood face banding. This flexible design works well for floor-to-ceiling installations that cover either all or part of a wall, and it can wrap around a corner, too.

The heart of my system is a simple plywood box, the same format upon which kitchen cabinets and bathroom vanities are built. All of these are designed as "units" of plywood boxes. Each one is built to different proportions with different combinations of shelves, doors, drawers, and countertops. You can assemble shelf units, kitchen cabinets, vanities, and other built-ins by following the same basic methods described here. ▶ ▶ ▶

Bookshelf Design

Good shelving not only complements its surroundings, but it also has structural integrity. No matter how pleasing the proportions of a built-in are, no matter how beautiful the finish on the woodwork is, your work will be a disappointment if the shelves sag or the cases rack when loaded with books. So when planning bookcases, always account for both appearance and strength.

Design strategies

First, let's focus on what the shelves look like as an interior design element of the house. Here are some strategies to keep in mind when integrating built-in bookcases with the rest of the house.

Think in units A wall of shelving is built as a series of vertical boxes constructed from plywood and solid-wood edging. Since the shelves are built in box units, design the shelving as a series of rectangles.

Complement the room Any built-in cabinet should fit in as a natural part of the room. Unlike furniture that will come and go, built-in bookcases will become part of the house—an interior feature as lasting as the window trim and baseboards. For this reason, I typically steer customers away from designing built-ins to match free-

BOOKSHELF PLANNING

Bookshelves are built in box units, so design the shelving as a series of rectangles, paying attention to both the vertical and the horizontal orientation of architectural features in the room.

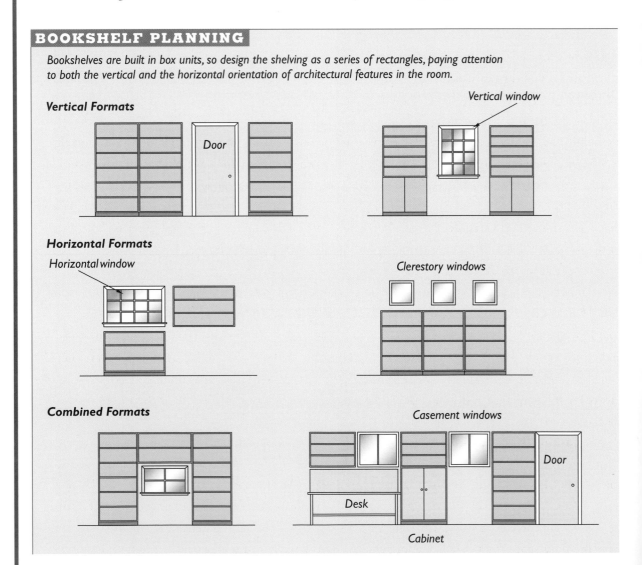

Vertical Formats

Door

Vertical window

Horizontal Formats

Horizontal window

Clerestory windows

Combined Formats

Casement windows

Desk

Door

Cabinet

Custom built-in shelves can accomplish many tasks. Here they serve not only as shelving, but as a plant stand and radiator cover as well.

standing pieces of furniture that will leave when the occupants move.

Often, bookcases run from floor to ceiling to maximize shelf space. In this case, it's not the overall box dimensions but the placement of the verticals and fixed shelves that reflect the room's elements. For example, I typically plan to have at least one fixed shelf in tall shelf cases (70 in. or taller) to stiffen the sides. Depending on the room's features, I put this fixed shelf at a height that matches the important horizontal elements in the room.

In addition to matching architectural shapes, try to match trim details. Back bands, fluting, and reveals on window and door casing can be mirrored in the face frame of the built-in. Even an arch-top window in the room may be repeated in an arch cut into the head of the bookcase. However, if you're ever in doubt about what will look good, err on the side of simplicity.

Accommodate furniture Bookcases must accommodate other furniture in the room. Often, this leads to a battle for wall space. If an entire wall is taken over by shelving, you won't be able to put the couch along that wall. Do you have the floor space for a couch, reading chairs,

tables, and other freestanding furniture to occupy the center of the room? Or do some of these pieces need to be pushed against the wall? If so, can the bookcases be built in units that fit around the furniture?

When planning all of this, don't forget that your house is an investment, both for yourself and for your family. Always weigh what will work for you and your particular needs against what will work in a general way for future occupants. The best design is a thoughtful balance of these considerations.

Shelf dimensions

Once you've identified the general design features, it's time to consider the specific layout of the shelves inside each case. Here you must account for what the shelves will hold, as well as for the strength of the materials you intend to use.

Case width The shelf span determines the case width. Pay careful attention to the structure so that the shelves won't sag. The sag of a shelf is measured as deflection, or the maximum distance at which the middle of a shelf bends under the weight of books or other items. The longer

The material and length of a shelf affect how much the shelf will sag—or deflect—when it is weighed down by books or other heavy objects. Deflections of 1/4 in. or more are noticeable. To reduce deflection, add hardwood banding, use stiffer shelving material, or decrease the shelf span.

Load

Shelf deflection
(should be less than 1/4 in.)

A variety of short and long shelves provides custom compartments and visual interest.

A fixed shelf length accents horizontal lines and ties two distinct areas together.

the shelf, the more it will deflect; the shorter the shelf, the stiffer it will be.

I aim for a deflection of no more than 1/4 in. across the length of the shelf. Therefore, the maximum length that a shelf can be depends on the strength of the materials you choose.

For example, if you use MDF without banding, the maximum length for a shelf is about 20 in. If you use 1x pine or plywood (also without banding), the maximum length for a shelf is about 34 in. Solid 1x hardwood can span up to 36 in. (See "Droop-Free Shelf Lengths" on the facing page for the free-span distance between vertical shelf supports.)

Regardless of the material you use, it's best to band the front edges with a 1x2 (nominal) solid-wood apron (preferably hardwood). In essence, the apron acts like a beam, doubling the load-carrying capacity of the shelf. An apron also gives the shelves some visual weight, too, which I think looks better.

Case depth A standard bookshelf measures 12 in. deep. This size holds most books, which range in width from 4 in. for standard paperbacks to 11 in. for binders and reference books. Large art books are often wider. Since the width of the material you use is a limiting factor, it's more

Droop-Free Shelf Lengths

Shelving Material	Without Banding	With 1x2 Solid-Wood Banding
MDF	32 in. (max.)	40 in.
Softwood boards or veneer-core plywood	34 in.	48 in.
Hardwood boards	36 in.	60 in.

Note: Assume that shelf stock is ¾ in. thick and that the shelves will carry heavy reference books. The maximum deflection is ³⁄₁₆ in. across the length of the shelf.

SHELF BANDING OPTIONS

Solid Wood
A nominal 1×2 hardwood apron adds visual weight to each shelf; when glued and nailed to the edge, it dramatically increases the shelf's load-bearing capacity.

Wood Moldings
This is often the least expensive option. Off-the-shelf moldings, such as ¾-in.-wide screen bead and 1-in.-wide lattice, can be applied with little effort—no planing or heavy sanding is required. Wider moldings lend visual weight to the shelves, but because these softwood moldings are thin, they don't significantly increase the strength of the shelves.

Plastic Strips
T-moldings and adhesive-backed strips can be installed quickly. I prefer T-moldings, which are inserted into a continuous slot in the shelf edge. Adhesive-backed strips can lose their adhesiveness and require additional gluing, which can be aggravating as well as time-consuming.

1×2 solid wood

Lattice

Iron-on (wood veneer or polyester)

T-molding

Ripping Plywood to Width

FOR A STANDARD BOOKSHELF UNIT, I try to make the finished shelves as close to 12 in. wide as possible in order to fit large books. Using nominal 1x2 hardwood shelf aprons and a face frame, my rip list for panel stock (MDF or plywood) looks like this:

Shelving Material	Width of Panel Rip	Width with 1xBanding
MDF	11⅛ in.	11⅞ in.
Case Stock		
End Stock	12 in.	12¾ in.
Scribe panel	13 in.	13¾ in.

TRADE SECRET

The widest solid stock (1x12) measures 11¼ in. wide. If a nominal 1x2 apron is added to the front edge, you can obtain shelves measuring a full 12 in. wide. Without the apron, however, the shelves will be narrower than those of standard bookcases. And if this stock is used for the sides of the case, the shelves will be narrower still.

economical to let oversize books hang past the edge slightly.

Case height I usually recommend that vertical cases extend all the way to the ceiling and tie into it with a cove or crown molding. Otherwise, you'll just build a dust trap on top of the case. In actuality, however, floor-to-ceiling bookcases aren't built to the exact height available. You must build the cases at least 2 in. shorter than the actual space so that the unit can be tipped into place and lifted up over the hanging rail without running into the ceiling (see "Use a Hanging Rail" on p. 148). The empty space will be covered by the fascia and ceiling trim.

You can build horizontal shelving to any height, depending on your needs. The top

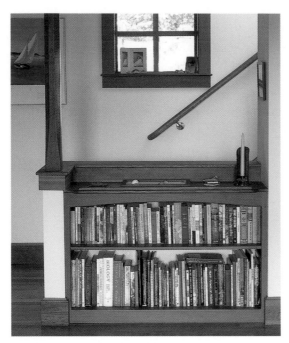

A simple but elegant built-in shelf makes efficient use of space and visually ties in with the room's wood trim.

might be a useful and needed counter area. Island bookcases can be positioned to screen or otherwise divide a room, while still letting natural light into the partitioned space. In those instances, look at the heights of windows and door headers, sills, sashes, countertops, and other prominent features in the room to determine whether they can be matched. The correspondence between casework and house features can pull together the entire design of a room, lending a degree of intentionality to your work that will be noticeable and visually pleasing.

Height between shelves Adjustable shelving provides a lot of flexibility when it comes to selecting the heights of individual shelves. I almost always design shelving so that most of the inside cases are supported by some kind of adjustable system, such as pins or tracks.

Regardless of whether the shelves will be fixed or adjustable, it's important to measure the books and other items you intend to place on

them. Then sketch out what might work. Books range in height from 6½ in. for short paperbacks to more than 12 in for reference guides. Most books are between 8 in. and 12 in. tall. Add at least 1 in. of extra space so that you have room to tip them out.

Fitting the space

To fit a bookcase in a room, you also need to consider the outside dimensions of the unit and figure out how much usable space there is in which to work. This sounds simple enough, but there's a catch: You can't simply measure the floor space and the wall area and then determine the overall dimensions. Rather, you must consider all three dimensions in relation to each other.

Here's an example to illustrate what I mean. One of the first large shelf units I built was for a rambling Victorian house. The room had 14-ft. ceilings, and the customer wanted bookshelves along an entire wall. No problem (I thought). I measured the floor and wall areas and marched off to build the cases. But I didn't check to see how plumb the walls were, how level the floor was, and how square the corners were. The bookshelves didn't fit . . . at all. Not only was the floor 1 in. out of level over 12 ft., but the walls were nearly 2 in. out of plumb over 14 ft. Because I had built my nice square cases to fit the exact floor space and the exact wall area, there was no way I could ever squeeze them into the room.

To avoid this problem, I have learned to do two things when designing floor-to-ceiling built-ins: (1) Map all three dimensions of the room and (2) based on the map, build the cases small and scribe the face frame to fit.

To "map" a room in three dimensions, start by checking the floor for level. If the floor is out of level from the front to the back of the shelving, you will be able to adjust for this when you set the kick base (see "Kick Base" on p. 146). If the floor is out of level along the length of the shelving, you must obtain an accurate assessment across the entire length, not just along the length of your level. Hold a 4-ft. level on a reasonably straight board. I find 1x2 strapping is the easiest to maneuver indoors, but any board that's long enough to span the room will do.

Also check the ceiling for level. If it is out of level as well, determine whether the ceiling "follows" the floor or whether it has its own sag. Similarly, check the walls for plumb and flatness. Assess the wall along the back of the shelving and on any sides into which the shelf will butt. If the shelves butt two walls at each end, try using pinch sticks to get an exact and easy measurement.

If all the walls and ceilings are wildly out of level and plumb, it's easy to get confused. To keep track of the directions in which the walls lean and the floors slope, I draw a picture of the entire area. If the area is especially large, or if I need super-accurate numbers, I set up a "string cross" (see "Mapping the Area" on p. 136).

Using pushpins in the floor and ceiling, stretch a plumb string line. Similarly, using pushpins in the end walls, stretch a level line between the walls. This provides a plumb and level reference from which to pull accurate measurements. The string cross is helpful for identifying "bellies" (or sags) in the floor and ceiling.

Once you have an accurate picture of the space, draw in the level and plumb lines that represent the edges of the built-in units (see "Mapping the Area" on p. 136). Give yourself plenty of leeway here. The unit should be at least ½ in. away from the walls and ceiling at all places. However, this means that there will be a much bigger gap between the walls and the ceiling in other places if the walls are out of plumb and the floor and ceiling are out of level. Not to worry. This gap will be filled in with a scribed face frame.

TRADE SECRET

When "mapping" a room, always start by checking the floor for level. Remember to check across the entire length, not just across the length of your level.

Measuring Walls

TO MEASURE THE EXACT DISTANCE between two end walls, use pinch sticks—two sticks that slide past each other until the ends hit the walls. Cut the ends at an angle so that they hit the walls at the long point. A pair of hatch marks across the two sticks marks the length. This method is especially helpful when you have to work alone.

Mapping the Area

IN OLD HOUSES WITH SAGGING FLOORS, drooping ceilings, and leaning walls, it's important to take your time to "map" the area for a built-in.

1. On a piece of paper, start with an ideal scenario (the dashed line) showing plumb end walls, a level floor and ceiling, and square corners. As you check the floor and ceiling for level and plumb, measure the discrepancies and note them on the map.

2. For large areas, it's sometimes helpful to set up a "string cross" secured with pushpins. This establishes a level and plumb reference from which to pull accurate measurements. Note that the cross does not necessarily need to be located in the center, but it should be positioned off the back wall just inside the face of the built-in.

3. Once you have an accurate picture of the walls, floor, and ceiling, outline the built-in. Make sure the outside of the case is at least ½ in. away from the wall. Note that the base of the built-in is 3½ in. up from the highest point on the floor. This leaves room for a kick space built on a level 2x4 platform. The shaded area represents the space that will be filled in with a scribe strip on each end wall.

Room length at ceiling

122 in.

+½ in. off plumb

Ceiling

+½ in. off level

Room height = 93 in.

Dashed line shows true level and plumb.

End wall

+½ in. off plumb

Room length at floor

121 in.

+¾ in. off level

String cross

Drive screw to anchor string

Strings out approximately 12 in. from back wall

Level string

Plumb bob

1½ in. clearance at low point

120 in.

Gap covered by crown

91½ in.

Shelves parallel to level line of string cross

Verticals parallel to plumb line of string cross

½ in. clearance

Building Cases

Once you have accurate numbers for the outside case dimensions, you're ready to build the unit. The bookshelf unit that I describe here has two main parts—the case, or plywood box, and the shelves that fit inside it. The face frame, kick base, and fascia are done later, when you install the bookcase. Let's start with the case.

Cutting panels

Begin by ripping all the panels for the cases and all the shelves from full 4x8 sheets. Plan to cut all the case panels (sides, tops, and bottoms) at once, using the same saw settings so that the pieces are consistent. In many ways, consistency is more important than exact, whole-number dimensions. Once the case panels are cut, rip the shelves $\frac{7}{8}$ in. narrower than the case panels to accommodate $\frac{3}{4}$-in. edge banding plus an added $\frac{1}{8}$ in. for adjustment. I usually wait until the case is assembled before ripping the back so I can get an accurate measurement of the actual for the back.

When using veneer-core plywood, pay attention to the orientation of the grain. The grain should run the length of the shelf to make use of the plywood's strongest dimension. MDF is equally strong in both directions, so grain orientation is not an issue.

PRO TIP

When cutting multiple parts, consistency is more important than exact measurements.

Typical Case Cut List

1. Side panels at wall:
  - Rip width to 12 in.
  - Cut to the height of the bookshelf, less the kick height.

2. Exposed (scribe) side panels:
  - Rip width to 13 in.
  - Cut to the height of the bookcase from the floor (including the height of the kick base).

3. Top and bottom:
  - Rip width to 12 in.

4. Fixed shelves:
  - Rip width to 12 in.
  - Cut the length to the inside width of the case.

5. Adjustable shelves:
  - Rip width to 11$\frac{1}{8}$ in. ($\frac{7}{8}$ in. narrower than case panels).
  - Cut the length to the inside width of the case, less $\frac{1}{4}$ in.

6. Back:
  - Rip the width to the outside width of the case, less $\frac{3}{8}$ in. (for each scribe panel).

Back

Top

Side panel

Scribe panel

Scribe strip

Banding

Shelf

Bottom

2×4 kick base

Finish kick

Face frame

It may sound redundant to say, "Wear safety glasses," but this advice bears repeating. Veneered plywood in particular splinters easily and throws back a lot of chips. Don't be caught blind without eye protection.

PROTIP

When routing the end of a board, pull the router into the board from each corner. Never push it out or you may split a wide sliver off the corner and ruin the edge.

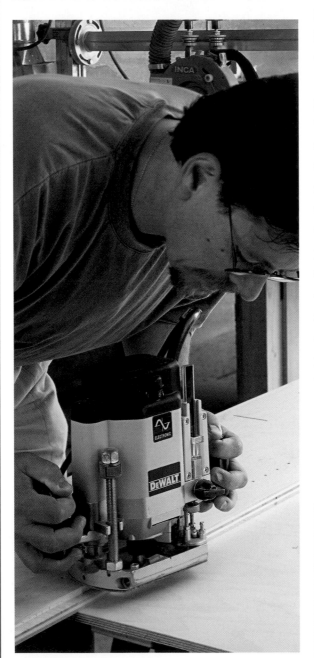

A rabbet can be cut with a bearing-guided router bit.

Side panels The side panels are the two vertical sides of the case. I cut two different types, depending on whether a side butts a wall or is exposed.

Sides that butt the walls are not visible, except inside the case. They are also shorter than exposed sides, because they don't need to cover the kick base. Sides that are exposed must be cut longer so that they cover the end of the 2x4 kick base, but they also need to be scribed to the back wall. I call these scribe panels.

I rip scribe panels 1 in. wider than other end panels (typically 13 in. wide instead of 12 in. wide). Then I cut a 3⁄8-in. by 1-in. step, or rabbet, along the back edge of the panel. I typically cut this step in two passes on the tablesaw. For the first pass, raise the tablesaw blade 1 in. above the table and run the panel through on edge (this task usually requires two people). For the second pass, lower the blade to just 3⁄8 in. above the table and run the panel through flat. If I'm working alone, I often use a router with a straight-cut router bit to cut this step. However, this creates a lot of dust, especially with MDF. A third (and probably easier) method is to use a dado blade on the tablesaw if you have one.

The step on a scribe panel provides a place on which to nail the cabinet back (typically ¼-in.-thick lauan plywood), leaving a 3⁄8-in.-thick "fin" that covers the gap created by the

When cutting full, heavy sheets of panel stock with a tablesaw, get help. Another set of hands to help you support the sheet is better than almost any table support system, unless you have a large shop and have room for an extra-large table.

hanging rail (see "Use a Hanging Rail" on pp. 148–150). In old houses, the back wall may be out of plumb or the surface out of flat. If that is the case, rip the scribe panel wider, so that the fin can be scribed to match the tilt and wave of the back wall.

Crosscut panels to length Once the panels have been ripped, I cut them to length, usually with a large sliding miter saw. I cut the case panels—sides, tops, and bottoms—first, then I cut the shelves to length. Most sliding miter saws can cut materials up to 12 in. wide, so they can easily handle the shelf stock, side panels, and top and bottom panels of cases. However, they don't quite cut all the way across wider scribe panels. For those, I usually cut as far as I can. Then, carefully supporting the cut, I slide the panel to the edge of the miter-saw table and finish the cut with a handsaw or cordless panel saw. Because of the difference in blade thickness between the miter saw and whatever else you use to finish the cut, there is often a little nubbin of material left. I use a utility knife or a sharp 1-in. chisel to very carefully pare off this bit

of material, leaving a single, clean surface on the cut end (see the photo below).

Of course, you don't need a sliding miter saw to make these crosscuts. You can also make them with a radial-arm or circular saw. I am not a big fan of radial-arm saws because I feel that they are too dangerous. But they have ample crosscut capacity for this type of work and cut with very little tearout, so many carpenters would argue that, in this case, they are the only practical choice.

Using a circular saw takes the most time, because you need to set up for each cut. Make sure that the panels are supported on both sides of the cut (I use a pair of 2x4s spanning a pair of sawhorses to support the panels along their full length). On veneered panels, you will probably have to score the cut with a utility knife to prevent tearout. For chopping shelves and the top and bottom pieces of the case, you will probably have to score both sides of the cut, since the end of one cut is the beginning of another on the next panel. This requires patience and precision. Using the thinnest sawblade with the most teeth helps reduce tearout. For a 7¼-in. saw, for example, use an ultra-thin 36-tooth blade. I find a 24-tooth blade on a cordless panel saw works well, too.

To prevent tearout, use a utility knife to score the cut deeply enough to break the grain at the surface.

TRADE SECRET

When using a circular saw or router to cut full sheets of plywood, support both sides of the cut with 2x4s. Rather than cut on sawhorses, I find it easiest to lay down four long 2x4s on the ground.

If the floor slopes out of level from the front to the back of the case, be sure to leave the exposed side panels long enough. I allow 4 in. to 4½ in. of extra length to cover the kick base. Since the kick base is built from 2x4s, which are only 3½ in. wide, this method provides an extra ½ in. to 1 in. for cutting the exposed panel to match the floor.

Tearout

Circular saw

Tearout up

Table saw

Tearout down

WOOD GRAIN THAT splinters along the edge of a cut is known as *tearout*. True to its name, tearout is the result of the saw's teeth coming out of the cut and tearing the grain as it leaves the wood. Tearout is predictable and likely to occur in these situations:

- **Orientation of the grain:** Tearout is always worse when crosscutting and minimal when ripping.

- **Solid wood:** Open-grained woods, such as oak and ash, are more subject to tearout than closed-grained woods, such as birch and maple.

- **Veneer:** All veneers are prone to tearout when they are crosscut. The thinner the veneer, the more likely it is to splinter along the cut.

Tearout usually occurs on only one face—the face where the blade exits. Therefore, the best way to avoid tearout is to support the grain on the "upcut" side of the cut, which depends on the rotation of the blade.

If the grain cannot be effectively supported, score along the cut with a sharp utility knife. When using a circular saw, you may need to both score the cut on one side of the blade and support the grain on the other side of the blade with a shoot board.

Prepping panels

After the panel stock has been ripped and chopped to size, I prep the panels by cutting slots for biscuits at the joints and drilling holes for shelf pins.

Biscuit joints There are two ways to secure fixed shelves and join the sides of a case to the top and bottom pieces: tongue-and-groove joints or biscuit joints (see the illustration below). I used to cut tongue-and-groove case joints, but now I use a plate joiner to make biscuit joints (see "Plate-Joining Techniques" on the facing page).

Start by marking the location of the biscuits on the inside face of each side panel. Measure the location of each intersecting panel (top, bottom, and any fixed shelves). With a framing square,

TWO CASE JOINTS

Tongue-and-Groove Case Joint
A table saw with a dado blade can cut this sturdy joint in a few passes.

⅜ in.

1/32-in. gap

Top

¼ in.

Side

Biscuit (or Plate) Joint

The modern biscuit joint is strong and quick to set up. Wood biscuits fit into slots cut by a plate joiner and swell on contact with glue, creating a secure and accurate joint.

Top

Centerline of biscuit approx. ⅜ in. from panel edge (location determined by plate joiner)

Side

Metal standards are nailed or screwed in pairs on both sides of each shelving unit. They are much more conspicuous than pins, but they are also stronger and generally much faster to install. They look best when let in to dadoes.

Shelf pins come in a wide variety of styles. I prefer the spoon type, which are the least conspicuous. All types fit into a series of holes drilled into the sides of the bookcase. Drilling the holes can be time-consuming.

Plate-Joining Techniques

THE FENCE AND BLADE HOUSING of a plate joiner have centerlines marked prominently in red, so layout is simply a matter of aligning this centerline with the centerline of the slot you want to cut.

1. The easiest way to lay out biscuits is to align the panels as they will be joined, then mark the biscuit that will hold them together with a single caret **A**.

While most plate joiners have elaborate adjustable fences, I rarely use one. Instead, I work right from my work surface. Without the fence, most plate joiners are set up to cut a slot about 3/8 in. up from the bottom of the tool—approximately in the middle of 3/4-in.-thick material. Keep track of which is the bottom and which is the top of each panel, because not all plate joiners cut a slot dead center.

2. To cut a biscuit slot in the edge of a panel, hold the plate joiner flat on the work surface and push the tool into the edge of the panel **B**. Keep all of the intersecting panels face up (as they will be installed), so that the slots will be in a consistent location.

3. To cut a slot in the face of a panel, I use a spring clamp to secure an angle jig to the side of the panel. The bottom of the plate joiner rides on the vertical leg of the jig. I always clamp the jig to the bottom of the intersecting panel so that the face slots align perfectly with the edge slots **C**.

draw a line on both sides of the intersecting panel. I use these intersection lines for aligning the faceplate jig when cutting slots in the face of the side panels.

Shelf-pin holes Once all the biscuits are marked and cut, it's time to make the shelf-pin holes.

1. Lay out the shelf-pin holes. I use a small tri-square and mark a line 2 in. in from each long edge of each side panel **A** (see p. 142). Mark the inside face of the panels; on scribe panels, be sure to measure from the step.

I usually space holes 2 in. apart and mark each with a crisp caret **B** (see p. 142). Starting from the top edge of the side panel, I begin my

PROTIP

Make a template from bead board to help locate shelf-pin holes accurately.

layout 8 in. down and end about 12 in. from the bottom. If I have fixed shelves, I stop and start the series about 6 in. on each side of the intersection lines.

2. Drill the holes with a brad-point bit to match the diameter of the pins (usually ¼ in. to ³⁄₁₆ in.) . Use a drill stop on the bit so that you can repeatedly drill to a consistent ³⁄₈-in. depth.

Laying out and cutting shelf-pin holes this way can be tedious work, and there are several jigs you can make or buy to speed the process along. But I find that if I'm building one case at a time, it's just as easy to lay out and drill by hand as it is to make and store a template.

Kick-space notch The final step in preparing the panels is to cut a notch for the kick space in the exposed side panels.

1. First, lay out the exact location of the notch on the inside of the end panels **D**.

2. Cut the notch with a jigsaw, making it 3 in. deep (that is, 3 in. from the face of the case) and 4 in. to 4½ in. high **E**. A Speed Square provides a ready-made guide for cutting. Make sure you leave the bottom of the side panel long so that it can be cut to the slope of the floor.

Assembling the cases

After the panels have been cut to size and prepped for biscuits and shelf pins, you are ready to assemble the cases. Once the glue begins to cure and the biscuits start to swell (this takes less than 10 minutes), there's no going back. So before you begin, make sure that you have everything you need on hand. This includes the following:

• Wood glue

• A wet sponge and bucket of water for wiping up excess glue

• A sharp chisel for scraping glue out of corners

• A charged cordless screw gun and plenty of 1⅝-in.-long wood screws (square drive preferred) for securing joints on panels that abut walls

• A nailer and 1½-in.-long nails for securing joints on exposed sides

Start by transferring the centerlines of all the fixed shelves to the outside face of the panel. This provides an exact location for screwing and nailing. Then you're ready to apply the glue.

Gluing the biscuits Assembling a case with biscuits is sort of like working with Lego® blocks—the pieces almost snap together. But you must work fast and remain focused.

1. Squirt a liberal amount of glue into each slot on one joint . Insert a biscuit and smear the squeeze-out along the joint. It's easy to apply too much glue (but important to apply enough), which is why it's imperative to have a sponge and bucket of water on hand.

At this stage, don't glue more than one joint at a time.

2. When the biscuits are firmly pressed into their slots, turn the panel on edge, align it with the end of a fixed shelf, and push the two meeting pieces together.

3. As the glue dries, the biscuits swell, which helps clamp the joint fast. Before that happens, make sure that you pull the two meeting pieces together and screw or nail them tightly together. If the side of the shelf unit will not be seen, it can be secured with screws, which hold better in the panel end grain . On an exposed end panel, however, use finish nails for a cleaner appearance H.

TRADE SECRET

While I prefer shelf pins because they are inconspicuous, an alternative to shelf pins is metal standards. These require routing two ¼-in.-deep channels into each side panel. This can be done on a router table or using a straightedge to guide the router in a straight line.

Fastening Panel Stock

BISCUITS PROVIDE THE STRONGEST connection between two panel pieces. Nails or screws supplement this fastening, but they are used mostly for holding the joint tight until the glue around the biscuit dries.

Use 1½-in. nails to clamp the joint on exposed faces. I typically use a pneumatic nailer, which drives the nail in one clean stroke. Driving nails by hand can knock the joint apart as you strike repeatedly with the hammer. If you do use a hammer, predrill the holes to minimize movement.

A better alternative to hand-nailing exposed faces is to use finish-head screws. These require more work to fill the holes over the screw heads. Drive the head about ⅛ in. below the surface. It's easy to strip out the small head, so predrill the holes and make sure you use the proper drive bit (a #1 Phillips-head or a small square drive).

Use screws on faces that won't be seen (for example, when they face a wall or another case). Screws grab better in the edges of all panel materials, drawing the joint tighter. I prefer using square-drive screws, which don't cam out as easily as Phillips-head drives.

Use 4d ring-shank nails (hand-driven) or narrow-crown staples (pneumatic-driven) to secure case backs.

4. After the first joint is glued and secured, all of the remaining joints must be glued with the panels on edge **I**. I glue all of the joints on one side panel first, then turn the side panel flat on the bench so that the attached pieces are sticking up in the air. Then I glue all of the remaining joints at once, lift the second side panel into place, and align each joint until the biscuits find their slots and fall into place **J**. This can be nerve-racking to do all at once, so it helps to dry-fit the second panel before glue-up so that you can be confident it will fit when the glue is on.

Installing the back At this point, all sides of the case are glued and secured. Lay the case on its front so that the back edges are pointing up. It's time to install the back.

1. Begin by squaring the unit: Measure the diagonal distance (from corner to corner) across the case, being sure to measure inside the step if you have one or more scribe panels **A**. Measure both diagonals, which should be equal. If they aren't, push the case around until they are.

CASE BACK DETAILS

The best way to join the back to the sides of a bookcase is with a rabbet, which holds the back securely in place. However, when the side panel is exposed, cut a scribe edge, as shown, and then glue and nail the back securely to the step.

Glue and nail to step

1/4 in.   1/2 in.   1/4-in. back   1/8-in. gap   3/8 in.   3/4 in.

13 in.   Shelf   11 1/8 in.   End panel

Scribe panel   12 in.

3/4 in.   1×2 shelf banding   Face frame

2. When the case is square, measure the exact width of the back and rip it to size. Then measure the length and chop it to length.

3. Once the back is cut, apply glue to the edges **B**. A continuous bead of glue is especially important along all of the back edges, so that books and other objects can be pushed hard to the back without opening an unsightly gap. Once you've applied the glue, carefully lift the back into place and nail it off **C**. I've found that, in addition to glue, headed ring-shank nails work best for securing the back to the case.

Installing Bookshelves

The method I describe here for installing bookcases has two essential components: a base and a hanging rail. The base is necessary for supporting a heavy load of books, and a hanging rail is important to prevent a full bookcase from being pulled over onto someone—a very dangerous possibility. But please note: I make my base and hanging rail in a special way, which I find works well. However, you should feel free to adapt these methods as you see fit. What is important is that you provide a sturdy base and a secure wall attachment for built-in bookcases.

Kick base

I typically install my bookcases on a kick base. That is, the bottom of the front face is recessed 3 in., much the same way in which kitchen cabinets are built. This is by no means mandatory. In fact, many customers prefer the base to be wrapped with baseboard, rather than having a recessed base as I describe here. You can easily adapt this method to your personal preferences. You can even build the recessed base and then wrap it with baseboard if you don't like the way

it looks. The important thing is that you build a level base for supporting a heavy load of books.

Begin by building a 2x4 ladder (see the illustration below). For a standard 12-in.-deep bookcase, I build this base about 8 in. wide and several inches short of the total bookcase length. It's much easier to build the structural base small so that it doesn't bump into old shoe molding and baseboard that may remain behind the built-in. If you have several units sitting side by side along a wall, build one "ladder" base for the entire run. This vastly simplifies the installation.

1. Start by snapping a chalkline on the floor where the front edge of the base will be. If the base is recessed, this line will be 3 in. from the front face of the unit. Refer to your 3-D map (see "Mapping the Area" on p. 136) to make sure that the case can be set plumb without running into the back wall higher up. If you're not sure, test-fit the location of the base by lifting a case onto the ladder base and checking for plumb.

2. When you're certain of the location of the front edge, level the ladder base and secure it to the floor with 3-in.-long wood screws. Be sure to check for level in both directions—along the length and from front to back. Shim the base with solid shims at each point where it is screwed to the floor. Use plywood blocks to build up any shim height greater than $\frac{1}{2}$ in.

3. Once you have the ladder base in place, you will know exactly where the bottom of your bookcase sits. Measure each end from the top of the base to the floor to determine where to make the final cut on the exposed panels (see the top photo on the facing page).

LEVELING BASE

Build a solid leveling base out of 2×4 stock. The base should be smaller than the footprint of your bookcase. A ¾-in. plywood kick panel can be applied over the front after the cases have been installed.

¾-in. plywood kick panel applied over kick base

2×4

Screw to floor; shim as needed

8 in. (for 12-in.-deep bookcase)

Length of base shorter than bookcase

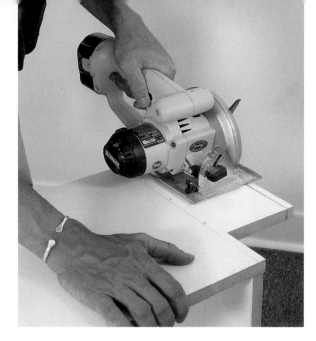

Scribe end panels

Before you secure the case to the wall, you may need to scribe-fit the end panels. If there is more than one case per ladder base, start by scribe-fitting an end unit.

1. Place the cabinet on the base and check for plumb. The step that was cut on the scribe panel prevents the unit from sitting in its exact location, so align it parallel to the front of the base, with the scribe fin pushed as close as possible to the wall. The panel may meet the surface at just one point, or it may meet in several places.

2. Choose the widest gap and set the dividers for that distance **A**. Then, holding this distance consistent, run the scribing tool along the surface, drawing a line onto the panel. This line will mirror the surface.

When scribing, consistency is everything. Hold the scribing tool at a constant position. I usually hold it parallel to a meeting surface (for example, level with the floor or ceiling when scribing a wall panel) and lightly rest my fingers on the wall to hold the scribe at a consistent angle as I draw **B**.

The bottom of a finished end panel should be cut to its final length in place. Although you can use a circular saw, a jigsaw tends to kick up less dust.

3. When you have a scribed line, cut the panel with a jigsaw. You may have to fine-tune the cut several times, holding the work against the surface repeatedly, resetting the scribing tool to the widest gap, and rescribing the line until you have closed every gap. A low-angle block plane works wonders for this fine-tuning work.

It is very important to leave exactly ¾ in. of material (the thickness of the hanging rail) at the level on the wall where the hanging rail will be installed. This can be tricky, but it's critical. If you don't have enough material here, you can end up

The Art of Scribing

SCRIBING IS A METHOD of transferring the contour of a wavy wall, ceiling, or floor surface onto woodwork. Once it is marked, the woodwork can be installed without any gaps showing. This method takes a lot of practice to do well, and your first few attempts may still require a little caulk (affectionately called "tube scribing") to dress out the joint.

To transfer the contour of a wall, use a drawing compass. Most carpenters I know rely on an inexpensive school compass, though many soon graduate to fancy wing dividers. The most important feature of any scribe tool is that the two legs can be securely tightened so that the distance between them doesn't change.

PRO TIP

A hanging rail may seem like an unnecessary extra step, but it speeds installation and keeps the case from tipping.

TRADE SECRET

To use a stud sensor, first calibrate the device over an empty wall cavity (an area of the wall that doesn't have framing beneath the drywall). When a calibrated sensor is moved over framing, it lights up, indicating that the signal has bounced back immediately from a denser material. Stud sensors don't work when foilfaced insulation materials (foam panels or batts) are used, since the foil reflects the signal evenly across the wall.

with a gap worse than the one you started with, and if you have too much, the hanging rail will hold the case higher than it should be.

Use a hanging rail

There are two big advantages to using a hanging rail. The first is a matter of safety. The rail prevents the bookcase from tipping over—no small detail, especially when there are kids in the house. The second is a matter of convenience for the installer. The rail makes it easy to attach the bookcase to the wall framing without riddling the back with screw heads. Also, because the rail spaces the back of the bookcase at least ¾ in. from the back wall, it allows you to bridge any surface irregularities that may pull the case out of plumb when you secure it to the back wall.

The rail that I prefer is commonly used by museums and galleries to hang heavy pieces of art. Hence, I typically refer to it as museum rail (see the illustration below).

1. To make the rail, rip a single board of ¾-in.-thick panel stock in half lengthwise at a 45-degree angle to create two pieces of rail stock **A**.

2. Use 1⅝-in.-long bugle-head wood v screws to attach half of the rail to the back of the bookcase with the long point of the bevel facing down **B**. The 45-degree angle essentially creates a hook that meets its mate, which is secured to the wall. The height of the rail is not critical. It should be in the upper half—preferably in the upper third—of the case. I try to align the rail with a fixed shelf to provide a good screw base. If that is not possible, glue the rail to the cabinet back.

3. Measure along the back of the case to find the exact height of the meeting rail—the half that attaches to the wall. Be sure to precisely measure this distance on the cabinet. Measure both ends of the case rail, and if it is slightly

MUSEUM RAIL

This type of hanging rail, commonly used by museums and galleries to hang heavy pieces of art, is made from a strip of ¾-in.-thick panel stock ripped in half lengthwise at a 45° angle. One length is attached to the back of the bookcase and the other to the wall, creating a kind of hook. Pay attention to the direction of the 45° angle when securing each length of rail.

45°

Rip lengthwise

Attach to bookcase

Attach to wall

45°

Wall

Case

skewed on the case, orient the wall rail accordingly. When transferring these measurements to the wall, measure from the top of the kick base.

4. Before screwing the meeting rail to the wall, locate the studs, either by sighting from existing nail locations or by using a stud sensor. Fasten the rail to the wall (long point of the bevel facing up) with 3-in. screws in every stud **C**.

5. Now you can lift the cabinet onto the base. Push the case until the two sides of the rail bump into each other, and then lift the case up and over the rail. Here is where the case height is most critical—that extra 1 in. to 2 in. provides enough leeway to lift the case over the top of the 45-degree cut. Once over and in place, however, it's there to stay. Finally, drive screws through the bottom panel into the ladder base to secure the case.

Finish kick panel

The finish kick panel can go on anytime after the case unit has been secured. I prefer using a piece of ½-in.-thick MDF, but it isn't really practical to buy a sheet of ½-in.-thick stock when you need only a few pieces. I often use ¾-in. material left over from building the cases.

If the cabinets run from wall to wall, the kick can be cut slightly smaller than the kick space height and scribed to fit. The gap at the top won't show unless you get down on your hands and knees. This gives you the room needed to scribe.

For high-end stain-grade work, I cut a miter on the exposed panel, which meets a miter at each end of the finish kick base to form a clean return.

Build the face frame

After the built-ins have been installed, you're ready to dress out the cases with a face frame and ceiling trim. Installing the face frame is finish work at its finest. This is when all the unsightly gaps in an out-of-plumb and out-of-level room are covered up and dressed out.

I typically use 1½-in.-wide stock to wrap the edges of the cabinet. However, on the sides that

FACE FRAME DETAILS

The ideal width for a face frame's verticals and fixed horizontals is 1½ in. The fascia, which overlaps the verticals across the top, is typically wider (approximately 2 in.). Shelf banding, which is often narrower than the face frame, is typically 1 to 1¼ in. wide.

Elevation — Head overlaps vertical — 1½ in. — 2 in.

Verticals run past fixed horizontals and bottom — Fixed shelf — 1½ in.

1½ in. — Kick panel

Vertical Section — Fascia wider than verticals and fixed horizontals

Horizontal Section — 1½ in.

butt into the wall, where the face frame will be scribed to match the contour of the wall, this trim may be slightly wider or narrower.

I always install the pieces in this order:

1. Start with the fascia, since all of the verticals butt into this piece. If a built-in extends to the ceiling, the fascia wraps around the open ends and may intersect with existing ceiling trim,

so you'll need to scribe to match the trim. To wrap the fascia, begin on the exposed side of the bookcase. Cut the side fascia long, trace (or scribe) the ceiling trim profile on the end, and then cut it out with a jigsaw **A**. After checking the fit and marking the length for the front miter **B**, cut the fascia to length and seal the end with adhesive caulk before nailing in place **C**, **D**.

2. Install the bottom rail .

3. Install the verticals that must be scribed to fit the side walls. Check the cabinet for plumb, hold the trim piece in place (being sure to keep it plumb, just like the cabinet), and scribe it .

Cut the scribed edge with a jigsaw and smooth the edge with a block plane .

4. Apply adhesive caulk to the case and fill in any open corners and gaps in the case. This saves time when preparing for the final coat of paint, because I am already aware of the blemishes and gaps that I found during the installation process.

5. Install the verticals at the edges of the exposed panels **J**, and fill in with the horizontal rails on the fixed shelves **K**.

6. The last step is to band the shelves. I like to use ¾-in.-thick hardwood, which provides a strong contrast against paint-grade banding on the case **L**. When nailing hardwood banding to the front of shelves, be sure to drive the nail straight, otherwise it will blow out on the face of the shelf.

DESIGN
OPTIONS

▲ **Floor-to-ceiling bookshelves incorporate cabinets that provide tidy storage for stereo equipment and a radiator cover (lower right).**

◀ **Built-in bookshelves can be used to create an alcove. The back of these bookshelves is made with tongue-and-groove bead board for a traditional touch that relates to the rest of the house trim. Note how the crown and baseboard tie in to the bookshelf trim.**

▼ **Built-in bookshelves along a hallway make efficient use of space. The bookshelf height matches the chair rail and countertop height.**

▲ **A low built-in bookcase creates a deep windowsill for a bank of windows. The wall baseboard ties in to the base of the bookshelf, and the shelf top overhangs like traditional window stool.**

▲ **Taking advantage of unused space makes sense for built-ins. The space below stairs provides a tall place for a built-in bookcase.**

BUILT-IN CABINETS

Custom-fit cabinets allow you to organize your home in ways that no bulky box purchased from a furniture store or office supply center can. A well-designed built-in accommodates your exact furniture layout while fitting seamlessly into the interior of your home, allowing you to recapture and use odd-shaped spaces, such as a triangular wall area underneath the stairs or beneath a sloped ceiling. You can also configure cabinets to create a partition or an island to divide interior living spaces, as well as add visual depth to walls with a window seat.

The built-ins I describe in this chapter are an elaboration on the basic box at the heart of the shelving described in the previous chapter. By adding doors, drawers, and countertops to this simple plywood case, you can create highly functional storage cabinets, window benches, and built-in workstations. ▶ ▶ ▶

Built-in cabinets can fill unused spaces, adding utility as well as decoration.

Upper shelf units situated above an enclosed base unit provide library shelving as well as a TV nook.

WHATCAN GOWRONG

Check television and stereo dimensions carefully before building a cabinet. Include a couple of inches of breathing room on each side of the equipment to help you slide the unit in and out when setting it up or connecting a VCR.

Designing Cabinets

One of the advantages of built-in cabinets is that they become an integral part of the house. You can build cabinets to fit the exact interior space, blend finishes with other woodwork, and shape and style the cases to reflect prominent architectural features in the room.

Built-in cabinets can serve myriad needs, including storage for games, art supplies, and household linens or housing for an entertainment system and the attendant CDs and DVDs. Adding a desktop or a benchtop to a series of cabinets creates an in-home workstation or a window seat. All of these can be built from a combination of modular plywood cases.

The method of cabinet construction that I describe here is often referred to as "case-component construction." The built-in cabinets are designed as a series of small, independent components—each one a simple plywood case—stacked or lined up next to each other, filled with shelves or drawers, and overlaid with doors. Typically built as frameless cabinets, the compo-

nents rely on biscuit joinery and European-style cup hinges and drawer slides. This type of cabinet has no stiles and rails to restrict access to the interior.

A combination of upper units and base units

Unlike floor-to-ceiling bookshelves, most of the built-in cabinets I install have a lower, or base, unit and a separate upper unit. Often, the upper units are open bookshelves, while doors cover the base units.

The division between upper units and base units typically falls at a height of 30 in. to 34 in. above the floor, which is a standard desktop or countertop height. The top of the base cabinets can be a solid-wood countertop, providing a

An elegant built-in cabinet visually ties in with the room's panel wainscoting while providing much-needed book-shelf and cabinet space.

strong band of natural wood that visually ties in with wainscoting and handrails. However, the divider between upper units and base units need not be one continuous countertop that separates open shelving from closed cabinets. In fact, variations in open and closed spaces can enhance a wall unit.

Door layout

In case-cabinet construction, the doors attach to the sides of the cabinet case or to fixed vertical dividers within the case. The door layout looks best when the upper and lower units align vertically. For example, notice how each of the shelf bays in the photo above mirrors the door layout on the base unit below it.

If the cabinet opening is wide, consider covering it with double doors. I avoid single cabinet doors wider than 2 ft., because they become ungainly to open and too heavy for standard hinges to support. If you're lining a hallway or upstairs balcony area with built-ins (see the photo at right), leave enough room for the door to swing fully open without running into a wall or balustrade.

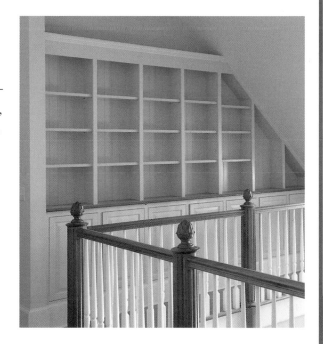

The height of the lower cabinets corresponds to the level of the handrail and wainscoting.

Building Cabinet Cases

As with the shelving cases described in the previous chapter, I build cabinet units from ¾-in. hardwood plywood. The top, bottom, and sides of the basic box are cut from full sheets of plywood and are butt-joined together with #20 biscuits. As described in "Case Back Details" on p. 145, I rabbet a scribe fin along the back edges of the sides that will be visible when installed, and this fin accepts the cabinet back. Sides that

PRO TIP

For a wide cabinet, use double doors. As a rule, any cabinet wider than 2 ft. needs double doors both for aesthetics and for relieving the strain on the hinges.

The sides of a fixed-shelf unit are prepped with a biscuit joiner. Note that a rabbet—a step that accepts the ¼-in. plywood back and leaves a narrow scribed fin— cuts along the back edge of each side piece.

A long run of cabinets is built from several units that are joined together.

butt walls are installed with a scribe strip, or the face banding is scribed to fit tightly to the wall, as described in the previous chapter.

Base units

Base cabinets are built as simple boxes that sit on a kick base. Not all base units are the same depth; indeed, the great advantage of building your own cabinets is that you can construct them to fit the space available. Nevertheless, a common depth is 24 in., a dimension that makes the most efficient use of panel stock.

I begin by ripping the panel stock to width. If I am using plywood, I rip the width to 23⅞ in. (half the width of a 4-ft.-wide sheet, less the kerf). If I am using MDF, I can usually rip to a full 24 in., since the sheets often come 49 in. wide (see pp. 22–33 for panel stock options).

I prefer to build base units no wider than 4 ft., a size that corresponds to an even multiple of 8-ft.-long panel stock and that is still relatively manageable. Make them much bigger than that, and the units become unwieldy. In general, when I lay out unit dimensions, I divide separate units into multiples of 2 ft. to conform to panel stock dimensions. However, when filling in an

Stretchers cut from 4-in.-wide plywood stabilize the front and sides of the cabinet case while providing a screw base for the countertop.

uneven length—say, 9 ft.—it often makes sense to build one 5-ft. and one 4-ft. unit. I try to keep unit lengths close to equal, and then build only one odd-size unit.

Cabinets wider than one set of double doors need a vertical divider to support doors in the middle of the run. These verticals are cut to the same dimension as a closed side panel and biscuit-joined to the bottom, as shown in the drawing on the facing page. Doors supported on

CASE CABINET CONSTRUCTION

A typical built-in cabinet consists of a base unit below a countertop, with shelf units above.

¼-in. plywood back

12 in.

Crown molding

Fascia to ceiling

Shelf pins at 2 in. o.c.

Plywood fins

#10 biscuits
(glued to upper shelf unit only)

5/4 solid-wood countertop

25 in.

Bullnose edge

¾ in. × 4 in. stretcher

Hinge baseplate

22 in.

Exposed
end panel
attached
with #10
biscuits

¼-in. × ¾-in.
hardwood
banding

Door

30 in.

Full-overlay
cup hinges

12 in.

Vertical divider

4-in. kick space

¾-in. plywood

34 in. to floor

End panel attached with 1⅝-in. screws

PRO TIP

Putting electronic components, such as a VCR, DVD player, or cable box, on open shelves makes it easier for the remote control to work.

fixed vertical dividers are hung on half-overlay hinges, while doors supported by end panels have full-overlay hinges.

Base units that will be covered by a countertop don't need a full-width top panel. Instead, I cut 3-in.- to 4-in.-wide "stretchers" to span the top of the cabinet, support the verticals, and provide a screw base for attaching the countertop (see the bottom photo on the facing page).

Facing

Once the cases have been built, I band the front edges. For plywood cabinets, I sometimes use iron-on veneer tape (see "Veneer Tape" on p. 171) to hide the edge grain. However, the

Top Treatments

CABINET TOPS CAN BE HANDLED in two ways. If the cabinet extends all the way to the ceiling, you can build a fascia, as shown in the drawing on p. 161. If the cabinet doesn't extend to the ceiling, you can, of course, simply trim out the top of the case with a simple cove or bed molding (shown below). A design that calls for wrapping the top with wide crown molding requires sufficient backing. The easiest way to do this is to build a separate top that slips over the top of the case, as shown in the drawing on p. 164. This design also provides a useful display shelf on top of the cabinet.

Using a plywood fin base allows in-floor heating vents to sit below the cabinet. The fins create a channel to redirect heat from the floor vent to a vent installed in the finished kick panel.

Plywood fins can be quickly installed on a cabinet (here, on the base of a case-style window bench). Use a framing square to align the fins, which have been predrilled for pocket screws.

tape tends to crack and peel at the edges if it is banged frequently. A ¾-in.-thick solid hardwood face frame holds up better over time.

Face framing is similar to that described in the previous chapter; however, it is attached to the cabinets before the units are installed. In this case, the unit doesn't need a fascia across the head. Instead, I glue and nail the vertical pieces so that they run continuously along the sides. These pieces are ⅞ in. wide; they cover plywood edges and leave a small (about ⅛-in.) overhang that can be scribed and planed so the units fit tightly together and to end walls. I make sure that the facing is flush to the inside of the cabinet and overhangs to the outside only, otherwise it may interfere with door hinges and drawer slides. Between vertical facings, I in-fill with 1½-in.-wide horizontal pieces along the bottom (flush with the top edge of the case's bottom panel) and 1¼-in.-wide horizontal pieces flush with the front stretcher (see the bottom photo on p. 160).

Kick base

I build the kick base from 2x4s (as described in the previous chapter) or as a series of plywood fins installed perpendicular to the face of the cabinet. If the floor is wildly out of level, I use a 2x4 "ladder," which I can level before installing the cabinet cases (see the drawing on p. 146). A level base is critical when installing any cabinet case and even more so when installing multiple units. If the units all sit on the same level base, it is easy to keep them square and aligned to each other. If the floor is level, however, the plywood fin approach is faster and more elegant. Instead of using pocket screws to mount the fins, you can build L-shaped brackets from small pieces of plywood.

Shims below the plywood-fin kick base level the case. After the case is secured to the wall, the shims will be cut back and a finish kick panel will be installed over the front of the fins.

A

B

Install fins or brackets every 16 in. to 24 in. o.c. to provide suitable backing for the kick panel and plenty of cabinet support. A 36-in.-wide base cabinet, for example, typically has supports beneath each end and in the center. Wider cabinets should have fins directly beneath vertical supports, as well.

Securing bases

Before securing bases to the wall and floor, I usually screw adjacent base units together.

1. Begin by planing the face frame for a tight fit between cabinets and against the end walls **A**. Then predrill through the edges of the face frame and clamp the cabinets tightly together before sinking the screws **B**.

2. Before screwing the cabinets to the wall, you need to find the studs. To quickly find the stud spacing, Clark Sargent pulls out his

To support wide crown on top of a cabinet, build a plywood cover that extends beyond the face.

¾-in. hardwood plywood

Crown

¾-in. × ¾-in. hardwood to match cabinet facing

Cabinet

PRO**TIP**

When a shelf unit will fit below a slanted ceiling, it's wise to leave a bit more material to scribe-fit.

Shelf cabinets often have fixed vertical shelf dividers corresponding to those on the base units beneath them.

tape measure and lays it across the back of the cases C.

3. Secure base units to the wall by driving 3-in. wood screws into each wall stud D. If the wall is out of plumb or out of square relative to the cabinets, shim between the wall and the case, or you may rack the cases out of square as you drive the screws home. Add a few judicious screws to hold the base. If the cabinet is on a ladder base, screw down through the bottom panel into the leveling base (which should already be level and secured to the floor). If the base units sit on a fin base, predrill the front edge and drive toe screws through the fins into the floor. Most bases are deep and not at risk of tipping over, so you don't need a lot of screws to secure a run of cabinets.

Shelf units

I make shelf cases in units and at the same width as their bases so that they align vertically. As I've mentioned in the previous chapter, I prefer to keep shelf spans short (under 2 ft. wide) to reduce the likelihood of the shelves bowing under the weight of heavy books or other items. This means that the shelf cabinets often need fixed vertical shelf dividers corresponding to those on the base units below. For verticals spaced no more than 24 in. apart, a ¼-in.-thick lauan or hardwood-faced plywood back provides plenty of strength.

For cabinets with adjustable shelves, I typically use the same shelf pins as those for bookcases (see the far left photos on p. 141). If the shelf unit is very tall, I usually try to install some fixed horizontal shelves for added strength. However, there

Drawer Construction

are times when fixed shelves are inappropriate to the design of a large cabinet, so I use knockdown connectors instead of standard shelf pins because they are stronger and help reinforce the cabinet. (See "Knockdown Hardware" at right.)

The facing for open shelves is also a full frame made from ¾-in.-thick solid wood. This, too, provides a much-needed scribe surface for seamlessly installing the units. As with the face frame on a base unit, I typically let ⅛ in. to ¼ in. of the face frame overhang the sides that butt unit to unit. When a shelf unit is installed below a slanted ceiling, it's wise to leave a bit more material to scribe the fit—at least ½ in. extra.

1. Before scribing, make sure that the unit is plumb **A**.

2. When the unit is plumb, scribe the face frame, holding a pencil flat to the ceiling **B**.

3. Remove the cabinet and plane along the scribed line, canting the plane toward the back to create a slight back bevel on the face frame **C**.

Most houses do not have enough drawers. That's because drawers take considerable time to build, so they are often used sparingly in a cabinet design. But where else can you conveniently store the myriad small items in your home? Even though they're time-consuming to build, it's worth including as many drawers as possible in a built-in.

Drawers also take a lot of abuse. Frequent opening and closing puts considerable strain on the box joints and the slide. However, if you are patient in cutting the pieces accurately, joining the box, and mounting the slides, a drawer will stay square and operate smoothly for a long time.

I use a simple but sturdy drawer design that can be reproduced fairly quickly. It's not the most elegant joinery, but once you've mastered the technique and understand the conditions necessary to make a drawer function well, you can enhance the design by cutting more elegant joints if you have the time, budget, and inclination.

Knockdown Hardware

KNOCKDOWN (OR KD) HARDWARE was originally developed in Europe, where homeowners typically take their kitchen cabinets and other modular cabinetry with them when they move. One of the most useful pieces of KD hardware is the Titus® connector for securing shelves. The connectors have studs that thread into shelf-peg holes, and the studs interlock with connectors inserted into 35-mm holes (drilled with the same Forstner bit used for cup hinges) on the bottom face of the shelves. Turning the connector draws the stud in tight, strengthens the shelf-case connection, and eliminates the gap between the shelf and the case.

Dimensioning drawers

Drawers must be built to precise measurements. If the drawer box is built even ¹⁄₁₆ in. too wide, the drawer may bind. Too narrow, and the slides won't fit together, or the drawer will operate with so much slop that it's bound to fail over time.

At issue here are the close tolerances that drawer slides require. Different slides require different amounts of clearance on each side of the drawer, so make sure you buy the slides before you start the project. Many slides require ½ in. of clearance on each side. I typically use European-style slides that require ¹⁷⁄₃₂ in. of clearance on each side, so each drawer must be 1¹⁄₁₆ in. narrower than the cabinet opening.

The inside of a 24-in.-wide cabinet made from ¾-in.-thick panel stock should be 22½ in. wide. Therefore, to use the European-style drawer slides, the outside dimension of the drawer box must be 21⁷⁄₁₆ in. wide (22½ in. minus 1¹⁄₁₆ in. equals 21⁷⁄₁₆ in.). (See the drawings below.)

A standard drawer depth for a 24-in.-deep cabinet is 20¼ in. This dimension works well with most three-quarter-extension slides, leaving an extra 2½ in. of empty space at the back of the cabinet for any wires and cables that may drop from a computer or stereo above. Even though you may not need this extra space, make sure you leave plenty of clearance at the back. A three-quarter-extension slide allows only three-quarters of a standard-depth drawer to roll out. Extra depth added to the drawer will not increase the opening but will be hidden drawer space left inside the cabinet, so there's no real convenience to adding drawer depth unless you plan to use full-extension slides.

Next, determine the height of the drawer box. This depends on the size of the drawer front you

DRAWER DIMENSIONS

To function properly, drawers must be built to precise dimensions. Here, the dimensions for a drawer in a 24-in.-wide cabinet uses drawer slides that require 1⁷⁄₃₂ in. of clearance on each side of the drawer box.

Plan View

Wall

21⁷⁄₁₆ in.

2½-in. space at back of cabinet

23-in. case depth

21⁷⁄₁₆-in. × 20¼-in. drawer box

20¼ in.

Drawer face

24-in. case width (22½-in. interior dimensions)

Section View

¼-in. clearance

⁵⁄₄-in. countertop

¾-in. plywood stretcher

¾-in. × 1-in. hardwood facing

¾-in. minimum clearance

Drawer face

3½ in.

Width of spacer

¼-in. clearance
³⁄₃₂-in. gap

Door

⁵⁄₈-in. plywood drawer box

have designed for the face of the cabinet. The drawer face typically rises ¾ in. above the top edge of the drawer box and hangs down about ¼ in. below the bottom of the drawer box. For example, a standard 5-in.-high drawer face (a standard-size drawer face at the top of a base unit) requires a drawer box that is 4 in. high.

Cutting drawer stock

I cut the bottom of drawers from ¼-in. hardwood plywood. I prefer smooth-faced birch with one A-grade face, oriented in the drawer with the grain running parallel to the sides. This slides into a ¼-in. by ¼-in. groove cut into the front, back, and sides of the drawer.

For the sides of my drawer boxes, I prefer to cut stock from ⅝-in.-thick Baltic birch plywood.

1. First rip the stock to the height of the drawer box (in this example, 3½ in.), and then rip the groove for the bottom ⅜ in. up from the bottom edge. A ¼-in. dado blade in a table-saw works best for cutting this groove. A down-cut spiral or a compression router bit works just as well but requires more time to set up. As a third alternative, I just make two passes through the saw with a standard ⅛-in.-thick carbide blade. Run a trial groove before ripping all of the drawer stock, and test-fit the bottom in case the plywood thickness varies.

2. Cut the sides, front, and back of the drawer box to length. Cut the sides full length (20¼ in.) and the front and back 1¼ in. shorter than the total width (20³⁄₁₆ in.) so that they fit inside the two sides (see the drawing on the facing page). Cut the plywood bottom so that it is ⁵⁄₁₆ in. longer and ⁵⁄₁₆ in. wider than the

The drawer bottom fits into ¼-in. grooves cut on all sides of the drawer box.

inside of the drawer box; this allows it to fit into the ¼-in. groove on all sides.

3. When all of the stock has been cut, you are ready to build the drawers. I screw the sides to the front and back of the drawers with 1-in. wood screws. Predrill holes through both ends of each side. Attach the sides to the front piece first, creating a U-shape, and then slide the bottom into its groove and attach the back (see the photo above).

Installing drawer slides and drawer faces

Most slides have a component that mounts in the cabinet and another component that mounts on the drawer. Usually, rollers are captured in a U-channel on one component; the other component has a flat surface on which the rollers move.

TRADE SECRET

For drawers below a countertop, leave at least ¾ in. of clearance between the top of the drawer box and the top of the cabinet. This allows the drawer to be tipped into and out of the slide without bumping into the stretchers.

WHAT CAN GO WRONG

Don't cut drawer pieces until you have built the cabinets. Plywood thicknesses vary, and cabinet pieces can shift slightly when the case is assembled. However, if you have already built the case, you can measure the exact opening required.

1. To mount the slide on the drawer box, turn the drawer upside down on your worksurface. Position the drawer component on the bottom edge of the drawer, flush with the front. Attach the slide with #6 pan-head screws, which won't interfere with the drawer's track. Elongated holes in the slides allow you a small amount of vertical adjustment. At this point, drive screws only in the center of the elongated holes so that you can adjust the drawer position later.

2. To mount the corresponding component in the cabinet, it helps to turn the entire case on its side. Measure the position of the slide on the side of the drawer box and add ¾ in. for clearance at the top. To simplify this installation, cut a spacer from scrap plywood to use for positioning the slide on the side of the cabinet. On the cabinet piece, elongated holes allow for adjustments back and forth. Again, only mount the slide with screws in the center of the elongated adjustment holes.

3. After the cabinet cases have been installed, install the drawer faces. Predrill four holes in the rough drawer boxes to hold the drawer faces **A**. Slip the rough drawer boxes into the slides so you can see where to place the drawer face. Hold the drawer face in place, using a scrap piece of 1x to gauge the ¾-in. clearance at the top of the drawer box **B**. Make sure that the drawer front is centered, with the same overhang on both sides, then drive the screws home **C**.

4. The last step is to check the travel of the slide and the reveal in the drawer face, making any final adjustments that may be needed. If the drawer rolls smoothly, no adjustments are necessary. But if the drawer bumps in its travel or jams, the slide positions need to be adjusted. Loosen the screws in the drawer channel and move it up or down, or loosen the screws in the cabinet channel and move it back and forth. When the slide travels freely without bumping or jamming, drive screws in two round holes in each channel. You don't need to lock in all of the screw holes; keep a few clear in case adjustments need to be made after the first heating season.

Countertops

Much of the time, a countertop for a built-in cabinet functions more like a mantel or a decorative shelf, not like the laminate countertops that you find in a kitchen. It often serves as the bottom of upper shelves that sit on a bank of door-covered cabinets.

Because this type of countertop doesn't get the wear and tear that typically occurs in a kitchen, it is a good place to use a handsome piece of solid wood with a natural finish. In this case, it can serve as a bold accent that visually ties the built-ins to wainscoting and handrails, as the countertop in the balcony built-in does (see the photos on p. 159).

I typically install the countertop after the base cabinets have been set and secured to the wall. If the countertop fits into a corner, don't assume the wall is square—it rarely is. Often the end must be scribed and cut at a slight angle to fit against the walls.

1. Begin by checking to see how square the wall is in relation to the cabinet, using a framing square and measuring along the front and back edges of the cabinet **A** (see p. 170). The goal is to find the longest dimension, then cut the countertop square to that length.

EDGE-GLUED COUNTERTOP

When gluing boards edge to edge to make a wide countertop, pay close attention to the orientation of each board to prevent the final piece from warping.

Bark side up   Pith side up   Bark side up

Flat-Sawn Lumber

Pith side to pith side   Bark side to bark side

Quarter-Sawn Lumber

This long countertop has been glued up from several pieces of 5/4 by 4-in. mahogany and given a bullnose profile along the front edge with a router-mounted roundover bit.

2. Set the countertop in place, scribing it to fit, if necessary, along the back and sides. When scribing a countertop or bench seat to an end wall, hold the pencil flat to the wall and maintain a consistent angle while drawing across the board **B** (see p. 170). If an upper unit will be installed on top of the counter, only the ends that butt into a wall need to be scribe-fitted; any gap behind the countertop is usually covered by the back of the upper cabinet.

PRO**TIP**

Allow a 1-in. to 1¼-in. overhang on the open ends of countertops that don't butt into walls. A flush end is difficult to align perfectly with the cabinet end, especially if the countertop must be scribed to fit.

3. For a straight cut, clamp a straightedge to the end of the countertop **C**. To avoid tearout on the top face, cut with the bottom of the countertop facing up. Also, it helps to have a helper catch the offcut so it does not split the corner when it falls.

4. Secure the countertop with 1¼-in. screws (for a ¾-in. top) or 1⅝-in. screws (for a 5/4 top), driven every 12 in. to 16 in. along the front and back ledgers on the base cabinets.

Doors

With European-style cup hinges, the doors overlay the edges of the cabinet case, rather than being inset in the openings of the face frame. This style is easier and faster to build, and because the hinges are adjustable, the doors operate smoothly with minimal effort (see "Cup Hinges" on pp. 173–175).

A more traditional look requires building frame-and-panel doors. As with wainscoting panels, real raised-panel doors are time-consuming to build. If I go this route, I some-times make a simplified version that is relatively fast and easy to construct (see "Simplified Frame-and-Panel Door Construction" on p. 172). Most of the time, however, I order true raised-panel doors that are manufactured to my specifications.

In its simplest incarnation, an overlay door is nothing more than a slab of hardwood plywood banded around the edges. Drawer faces can be fashioned from the same materials, so the front of the cabinet becomes a smooth, seamless plane with a ³⁄₁₆-in. gap between the doors and the drawer fronts.

Cutting doors

The first thing I do when making solid ply-wood doors is calculate the size of the doors and drawer faces. For the door width, I measure the width of the cabinet case (outside to outside) and subtract $\frac{3}{8}$ in. ($\frac{3}{16}$ in. is the width of the gap between doors) from each side of each door. Then I subtract for the thickness of the band-ing—$\frac{3}{32}$ in. for veneer tape and $\frac{1}{4}$ in. for hard-wood. Similarly, for the door height, allow for a $\frac{3}{16}$-in. gap between the top of the door and the bottom of the countertop or drawer face, and don't forget to subtract for the banding thickness when chopping the door to height.

Often, the trickiest part of cutting doors comes in the planning stages. Determine the plywood division so that you can get the most out of each sheet of plywood (for more on cut-ting plywood efficiently, see the bottom drawing on p. 13). When I know the plywood division, I rough-cut the door into manageable slabs with a straightedge and a circular saw, then cut to the final dimensions on a tablesaw.

Banding

Plywood doors must be banded along the edges to hide the edge grain. The easiest way to do this is to use iron-on banding, or veneer tape. While this material is relatively inexpensive and easy to install, it is fairly delicate and often starts to separate after a few years of use, particularly if the edges are knocked or pulled. More often, I apply iron-on banding to the edges of the cabinet case behind the doors and use $\frac{1}{4}$-in. hardwood edging for the doors. Solid-wood banding takes time to apply well, but it is very durable over the long haul. I also like the look of a painted wood door with a natural wood accent around the edges.

Veneer tape This hardwood veneer with heat-sensitive adhesive comes in rolls slightly wider than the edges of $\frac{3}{4}$-in. plywood. It can be applied with a banding iron, available from some woodworking supply houses, or with a normal household iron (I bought one at a yard sale exclusively for this use) on dry (no steam).

1. Begin by cutting lengths of veneer tape about 1 in. longer than the width of all the doors. I apply the tape to each side first, trim it, and then apply it to the top and bottom edges. Hold it on the edge and press down firmly with a hot iron until the glue softens (you can see it bubble around the edges). If you move too slowly, you can scorch the veneer; too fast, and the tape peels off. With practice, you'll find the right pace.

2. After the adhesive cools, cut the ends of the tape flush to the corners with a utility knife and plane the edges flush to the faces.

Apply veneer tape with a hot iron. After the adhesive cools, cut the ends of the tape flush to the corners with a utility knife and plane the edges flush to the faces.

Simplified Frame-and-Panel Door Construction

FRAME-AND-PANEL DOORS WERE invented to solve the problem of wood movement. A solid-wood panel pinned in a frame will soon crack. In frame-and-panel construction, the panel "floats" in the frame, expanding and contracting as necessary. I make fill panels out of MDF, which is very stable and doesn't expand and contract with seasonal changes in humidity. Therefore, my frame-and-panel doors are decorative rather than practical.

My modified design uses a 1x4 frame made of maple or poplar and an MDF fill panel.

1. I begin by ripping 1x6 poplar in half to get 2¾-in.-wide rail and stile stock. Then I cut a ½-in. by ½-in. rabbet along the milled edges of each board.

2. I butt-join the pieces with the rabbet facing the inside of the frame and the ripped edge on the outer perimeter.

I usually build frames approximately ½ in. larger in both directions and then trim them to the exact size on a tablesaw, using a jointer or a plane (hand or power) to smooth the cut edges. I'm careful not to cut the exposed face of the rails less than 1¾ in. wide; otherwise, cup hinges won't fit. When joining the stiles and rails, I cut a rabbet in the ends of the stiles that matches the rabbet on the rails. Although I use a tablesaw to cut the rabbet on the rails, I typically crosscut the rabbet on the stiles with a power miter saw equipped with a depth stop.

3. The last step is to cut a fill panel from ⅝-in.-thick MDF. I cut the panel ¼ in. undersize and rout a small cove along the perimeter. This panel "floats" in the frame and is secured with a light bead of adhesive caulk and ½-in. brads nailed from the back through the rabbet.

To cut a door to its precise dimensions, trim it to the exact size on a tablesaw, and then smooth the cut edges by running them through a jointer, as shown here.

Section

- 2¼ in.
- Adhesive caulk
- ¼-in. cove
- ¾ in.
- ½ in.
- ⅝-in. MDF
- 2¾ in.
- ½-in. brad
- ¼ in.
- ¾-in. poplar or maple
- ½ in.
- ½ in.
- ¼ in.

Door face

1¾-in. minimum

Door back

Simple Frame-and-Panel Door
Elegant paint-grade cabinet doors can be made with a hardwood frame and an MDF in-fill panel.

Solid-wood edging I prefer to cut solid edging from ¼-in.-thick strips of hardwood.

1. First, joint the edge to smooth off any saw marks, then run the board through the tablesaw. This gives you strips with one smooth edge that faces out and one sawn edge that faces the door edge.

2. Apply these strips along the top and bottom edges of the door first, trim them to the width of the door, and then run the side banding continuously over the ends of the top and bottom edges. When applying the strips, use yellow carpenter's glue and nail every 6 in. with ½-in. to ¾-in. brads.

Cup hinges

Cup hinges are the secret behind frameless built-ins. These innovative "Euro-style" hinges remain completely hidden when cabinet doors are closed, giving the cabinet front an uninterrupted, uncluttered face. Compared to leaf hinges, cup hinges make hanging cabinet doors much easier,

CUP HINGE TYPES

With different size baseplates, cup hinges can accommodate a variety of cabinet door styles.

Full Overlay — Case side, Baseplate, Hinge, Cup, Door

Half Overlay — Vertical divider, Baseplate, Hinge, Cup, Doors

Inset — Case side, Baseplate, Hinge, Cup, Door

Cup Hinge Swing

CUP HINGES ARE DESIGNED TO MOUNT on the inside face of a cabinet door. The most common configuration for full-overlay doors allows the doors to open to an angle of 110 degrees to 130 degrees. Cup hinges can usually be converted to work for half-overlay doors by using a spacer, or for inset doors by using a new baseplate. A wide variety of specialty types are also available for doors that swing up to 175 degrees, as well as for extra-thick doors, blind-corner doors, and glass doors.

When choosing the opening angle of the hinge, consider where the cabinet is placed. For wall cabinets, a 120-degree hinge works best, allowing an unobstructed opening of the entire cabinet. For base cabinets, I use hinges that open to 165 degrees. This permits the door to open almost flat against adjacent cabinets and prevents the door from being ripped out if it's left open and someone runs into it. For base cabinets against a wall, I use hinges that open to 110 degrees to prevent the door from hitting the wall.

Some cup hinge manufacturers have added a snap-on feature that allows you to mount or dismount the door without tools. You simply pull a small lever to release the door. This means that when it's time for a plumber to replace a sink trap or service the disposal, you can quickly remove the sink cabinet doors and set them aside.

The "cup" side of the
hinge mounts in a 35-mm
round mortise bored into
the inside face of the door.

The baseplate mounts to
the side of the cabinet at
a precise distance from
the top and front edges
of the case.

as long as you have the right tools. The biggest advantage is that cup hinges can be adjusted after they have been installed, allowing you to evenly space the gaps between the doors. Cup hinges work equally well with all door styles, and some even work on face-frame cabinets.

Cup hinges have two parts: a cup, which mounts on the inside face of the door, and a baseplate, which screws to the side of the cabinet case. The weight of the door is distributed over the entire rim of the cup, which makes for a relatively strong hinge compared to a traditional leaf hinge, which puts all of the door's weight (and that of a child who might swing on it) on just a few screws. The collapsible arm attached to the cup slides onto a baseplate that can be adjusted about ⅛ in. in three directions: up, down, and sideways. Conventional leaf hinges have no adjustment capability, so you not only need to be dead on when you install them, but you also have no recourse for readjusting the hinge over time.

Some hinges come with 7.5mm "Euro" screws, a larger-diameter screw designed specifically for particleboard. Or they may come with nylon inserts that fit into even larger holes and accept a standard #6 screw. Nylon inserts are probably the best option for particleboard, because they allow the screw to be removed and replaced many times.

Installing cup hinges is a two-step process: The cup, which holds the hinge arm, is mounted on the door, and the baseplate is mounted on the case.

1. Drill a 35mm-diameter hole for the cup part of the hinge on the door using a special Forstner bit. The carbide Forstner-style bit

The cup is bored with a 35-mm Forstner-style
bit, creating a clean, flat-bottomed hole with
no tearout at the surface.

Tips for Using Cup Hinges

- Always test the hinge placement by mounting both parts of the hinge on two pieces of scrap plywood before mounting the hardware on a cabinet.

- Make the height of doors greater than the width.

- Keep hinges as close as possible to the top and bottom edges of the doors—a maximum of 3 in. is recommended

- Don't exceed the maximum cup drilling distance from the edge of the door. This will cause the doors to bind.

- Attach the baseplate using all available screw holes—a great deal of force is applied to the plate when the door is opened and closed.

- Make sure that the hinge arm is square to the edge of the door. Improper mounting makes it harder to open the door and could eventually cause the hinge to fail.

- Don't overuse hinge adjustments. If you need to make excessive adjustments, check your mounting jigs and measurements.

Adjust cup hinges with a Pozidriv® screwdriver to make the gap between the edge of the door and the rail or adjacent door equal and parallel.

severs the fibers at the perimeter of the mortise while also cutting with a sharp knife-edge along the bottom. The result is a clean, flat-bottomed hole with no tearout at the surface. The hole should be drilled to the depth of the bit head—about ½ in. Not all bits have a lead point, so unless you have a drill press, you will need to make a jig to guide the bit. Then install the hinge on the door.

2. Mounting the baseplate requires careful positioning on the cabinet side. You can make your own jig for this or buy one from the hinge manufacturer. To make the job easier, tip the cabinet on its side, so gravity works in your favor. Use #6 ⅝-in. oval-head sheet-metal screws. Unlike wood screws, sheet-metal screws have a consistent shaft diameter, so they maintain a better grip in MDF and particleboard.

Every brand of hinge has its own method of adjustment. Some hinges are adjustable in two dimensions, others in all three dimensions. The screw that is the farthest back adjusts the height, so loosen it to move the hinge up or down. The middle screw enables you to adjust the door in or out to align the front face of the doors. The outermost screw adjusts the hinge sideways to equalize the gap between adjacent doors. Loosen it to move the door away from the baseplate; tighten it to move the door toward the baseplate.

PRO**TIP**

When working with European-style hinges, use a special Pozidriv screwdriver available from hinge suppliers. A standard Phillips-head driver will ruin the screw heads.

DESIGN
OPTIONS

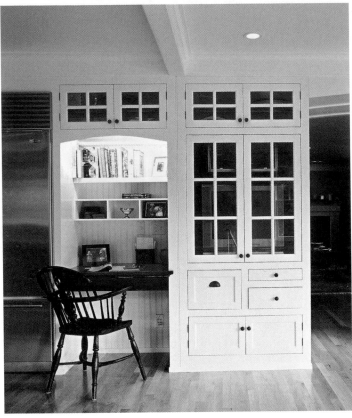

▲ A desktop, rather than a base cabinet, is a useful alternative in a kitchen bank of cabinets. The desktop, which extends past the plane of the cabinets, laps onto the cabinet face sides—a pleasing resolution for joining naturally finished hardwood with painted wood.

▸ In this recessed bank of cabinets, wide 1x4 vertical rails create an even spacing between the square transom cabinets along the top. The verticals on the outside continue uninterrupted all the way to the baseboard to frame the composition, while the two verticals on either side of the open center shelf are interrupted by the countertop. The center vertical creates the apex of a triangle formed by these verticals that provides a strong accent to the overall symmetry of the units.

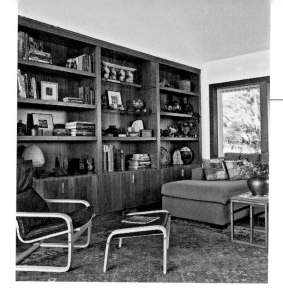

This built-in cabinet/bookshelf consists of three units, each built separately and installed side by side. Solid cherry verticals cover the joint between the units.

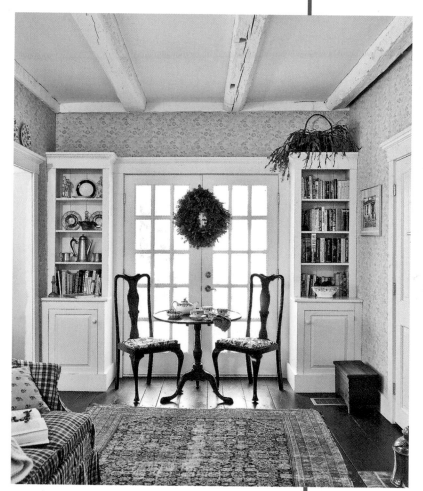

▲ Two cabinet/bookshelf units flanking French doors create an intimate seating alcove. The countertop height matches the center rail of the door, which unifies the built-ins with the rest of the room.

GLOSSARY

A

Apron The flat wall trim below a windowsill; the bottom piece of window casing.

Architrave In classical architecture, an architrave is the beam that extends across the top of the columns. It forms the lowest part of the entablature, and it is used to describe the trim across the head of a window or door, especially one built up to evoke a classical architrave.

B

Back band An L-shaped molding used to dress the outside perimeter of door or window trim.

Backer Any material used behind trim to provide a surface to nail to. With trim, it's used specifically to provide nailing for attaching crown molding and wainscoting. The terms *backer* and *blocking* are often used interchangeably.

Backing out Cutting out the material behind the front mating edge of a miter or coped joint so that only the material at the front edges touches. If a cut is not sufficiently backed out, the joint may not close tightly.

Back priming Painting the back side of a board with a primer to seal it against moisture.

Banding Applying a strip of wood to the edge of a shelf to hide the plywood edge and create a thicker appearance at the edge. A solid wood band resists bending; the longer the shelf, the wider the band should be.

Base cabinet A lower cabinet that sits on the floor, usually beneath a countertop.

Base cap The molding applied to the top edge of baseboard.

Bead joint A raised joint between two pieces of trim created by applying thin, rounded molding between the two pieces.

Bed molding A molding placed between the ceiling and the wall similar to a crown, but typically smaller. The term bed molding traditionally refers to an exterior molding, but it can be used indoors, as well, as part of a built-up cornice or architrave.

Bevel The angled cut on the end, or along the edge, of a piece of material. An angled cut is referred to as a "bevel" when it is along the edge or end (through the thickness) of a board and as a "miter" when the cut is across the face (or width) of the board.

Bevel square A hand tool with an adjustable blade used to transfer a bevel or miter angle.

Bevel board A jig made to measure the angle of a bevel or miter; it consists of a small board onto which the precise lines radiating from a single point of the edge have been drawn.

BF (board foot) A unit measurement for wood equal to 1 ft. by 1 ft. by 1 in. Rough-sawn lumber is typically sold by the board foot, while dressed lumber is usually sold by the linear foot.

Birds-eye Refers to the figure in wood grain that appears as a group of small ($\frac{1}{8}$ to $\frac{3}{8}$ in. in diameter) swirls or blisters thought to resemble little "eyes." Birds-eye figure is most common in sugar maple.

Biscuit A football-shaped spline that fits in a slot in the edges of two boards to invisibly join two boards.

Block plane A small handplane specifically designed to smooth end grain.

Blowout The mishap caused when a nail that is placed too close to an edge pushes out and mars a finish surface.

Bow Distortion in a board describing the curvature in the face of a board along its length. A bow is distinguished from a *hook*, which is a curve along the edge of a board, or

a *cup*, which is a curve in the face running across the width.

Book-matched veneer Face of plywood created with flat-cut veneers that have been paired from two thin sheets of veneer (called "flitches") cut from adjacent pieces in a log.

Butt joint The joint between two square-cut pieces of wood.

C

Capital The crown or top of a column. The term is often used to describe the top of ornate window and door trim.

Casing The trim used to "case," or surround, a window or door. Casing is applied between the window or door *jamb* and the wall.

Chair rail Horizontal molding applied to a wall about 3 ft. to 4 ft. above the floor.

Check A defect in lumber caused by the separation of the annual growth rings, usually at the ends, and most visible in end grain.

Chopsaw Common term for a power miter saw. In commercial work, a chopsaw specifically refers to a saw that uses an abrasive blade to chop steel channel and pipe, but it has been adopted for use by trim carpenters to refer to their miter saws.

Clamshell A small, inexpensive trim used for windows and doors milled with one thick edge that tapers to a thin edge.

Conditioned wood Lumber that has been allowed to sit, or acclimate, to the temperature and moisture conditions where it will be installed. Using conditioned wood results in fewer problems due to shrinkage or expansion.

Coped joint Joint made by cutting along the profile of a molding, allowing the profile on one piece to mate with the profile on the other.

Coping saw A handsaw used to cut *coped joints.*

Corner block Square block used to join the top corners of window or door *casing.*

Cornice An elaborate crown between the wall and the ceiling, often built-up from multiple pieces of molding.

Countersink To set the head of a screw flush or below the surface of a board.

Counterbore The hole drilled to allow the screw to be set below the surface of a board.

Cove A molding with a concave, semicircular profile.

Crown The trim between a wall and a ceiling. A smaller crown is sometimes made with *bed moldings,* while a larger crown built-up from multiple pieces is often called a *cornice.*

Crossbands The veneer layers in plywood that make up the core (distinguished from the face *veneer*).

Cup (or cupping) Distortion in a board across the width of a board. Cupping is caused by the board absorbing more moisture on one face, so it expands more on one face than on the opposite face.

Cup hinge A European-style door hinge commonly used for cabinets that is installed in a 35mm or 26mm hole, or "cup."

D

Dado A wide groove cut across the width of a board to accept the end of another board. Often a dado is cut wide enough to receive the full thickness of the joining board.

Dentil A square block cut in series—said to resemble teeth—in a *cornice* molding.

Dimensional lumber (dressed lumber) Cut lumber planed to a finish dimension usually measuring less than its *nominal size.* For example, a 1x4 measures ¾ in. x 3½ in.; a 1x6 measures ¾ in. x 5½ in.; a 1x8 measures ¾ in. x 7¼ in., etc.

Double plate Second horizontal plate added to the top of a wall frame, over the first top plate. This plate is needed to tie the top of a stud wall together, but it may also provide good nailing for ceiling moldings and backer.

E

Elevation view The geometrical projection of the vertical face of a building or interior.

Equilibrium moisture content Moisture level in wood that matches the moisture level in the surrounding air. The goal of acclimating wood to jobsite conditions is to reach this equilibrium.

F

Face frame The frame surrounding the door on the face of a cabinet. In a face-frame cabinet the doors and drawers are inset into the frame, as distinguished from a frameless cabinet, which has doors and drawers that overlay the edges of the cabinet box.

Fascia The horizontal finish board installed at the ends of roof rafters. May also refer to trim used to tie together the top of a series of cabinets.

Finger joint A series of "fingers," or splines, machined on the ends of two pieces of wood. When the joint is finished, these fingers mesh together and are held firmly with an adhesive. Using this type of joint, it's possible to make a long piece of mill stock with many short pieces of wood.

Finished stringer The trim board that sits above the treads to provide a *kick base* that ties into the baseboard at the top and the bottom of the stairs.

Flitch Among lumber dealers, it refers to a section of a log cut on opposite faces, leaving two waney edges. It is also used to describe veneer. In this case, it typically refers to a bundle of sheets that are all flat-cut from the same section of a log. This type of *veneer*

is distinguished from the curling spiral of veneer produced from rotary cutting.

Forstner bit The style of drill bit guided by a cutting edge around the perimeter. Typically used for boring a flat-bottomed hole, or "cup," for a cup hinge.

G

Grade Lumber is graded according to the number and size of defects, including *knots,* holes, *pitch pockets,* and missing pieces on the edges or corners, called *wane.*

Clear select Denotes the top grades of lumber; usually free of any defects.

Grain (texture) The growth patterns of the fibrous tissues in wood.

Close grain (fine grain) Wood with narrow, inconspicuous annual rings.

Cross grain Any grain that deviates from the line parallel to the edge of a board. Often used to describe the direction of cutting or planing a board perpendicular to the grain lines on a board.

End grain The ends of the fibrous cells that are exposed at the end of a crosscut board.

Flat grain The grain in lumber that has been sawn parallel to the core (or pith) of the log and tangent to the growth rings. This results in the growth rings running at an angle of less than 45 degrees with the surface of the board. Flat-grain hardwood and specialty softwoods are often designated CMG, or clear mixed grain.

Open grain A designation common among painters and finishers for describing woods, such as oak, mahogany, and ash, with large pores in the grain structure.

Vertical grain (edge grain, quartersawn, plain sawn) Typically designated as CVG (clear vertical grain) by hardwood dealers, vertical-grain lumber is cut from the log where the growth rings are running vertically, or close to vertical, through the thickness of the board. The result is usually the most stable grain configuration in relation to the geometry of the board.

H

Heartwood The darker grain in a board that is cut from the inner, central core, or pith, of the tree. The denser heartwood consists of dormant cells that ceased to carry sap at the time the tree was cut. Compare *sapwood.*

Header (head) Usually the structural beam over a window or door opening. Carpenters may also casually refer to the head trim over an opening as the header or header trim.

Hook Distortion in the edge of a board along its length. A hook (sometimes also called a "crook") is distinguished from a *bow,* which is a curve along the face of a board, or a *cup,* which is a curve in the face running across the width.

Horns The notched end of a window stool that extends under the trim on the side of the window.

J

Jamb The vertical surrounding of a door, window, or mantel opening. The jamb runs perpendicular to the casing, which it intersects.

Extension jamb An additional trim piece that may be necessary to extend a window jamb so it ends flush to the wall.

Jigsaw A power saw with a narrow, straight blade that runs up and down. Typically used to cut around curves and coped joints.

Joist The framing members in a floor or ceiling.

K

Kerf or kerfing The path cut by a saw blade. When calculating the dimensions of pieces cut from a board or panel, it is necessary to account for the kerf, which will be turned to sawdust once the saw runs through it, but won't be included in the final dimension of the board.

Kick base The bottom of a cabinet that sits on the floor. Typically the kick base (often simply called the kick) is recessed behind the front face of the cabinet above it.

Knot A dense cluster of cross-grained wood where a branch grew in the tree the board was cut from.

Loose knot A knot formed by a dead branch of the tree. As the tree continued to grow around the dead branch it trapped the dead cells, which can make the knot prone to fall out. When a loose knot falls out, it creates a knot hole.

Sound knot A knot that is solid across its face, at least as hard as the surrounding wood, and shows no indication of decay.

Pin knot Very small, tight knot; defined by lumber graders as any knot less than ½ in. in diameter.

Spike knot A knot cut nearly parallel to the long axis of a branch, so that the exposed section of grain is elongated.

L

Laminate Any product made by bonding two or more layers (laminations) of material. Specifically, it often refers to the thin plastic sheet material used as the top lamination on a countertop.

Lauan A type of mahogany used for making thin plywood. Standard lauan ply measures about ³⁄₁₆ in. thick (¼ in. nominal) and comes in 4x8 ft. sheets.

LF (linear foot) A measurement in feet along the length of the board, regardless of the board's width. May also be applied to a run of cabinets, wainscoting, and so on.

Long point The sharp end of a miter.

Lumber core plywood A high-grade veneered panel stock with a core made of solid strips of wood (usually basswood).

M

MDF Medium-density fiberboard, made from a fine wood flour mixed with an adhesive binder and heat-pressed into panel stock, boards, or moldings.

MDO Medium-density overlay, a high-grade fir plywood surfaced with a heavy-weight paper. Favored by sign makers, it takes paint extremely well and is rated for exterior use.

Melamine A thermally fused, resin-saturated paper finish that's typically laminated over a particle-board core.

Millwork Any wood milled to dimension for woodworking. Architectural woodwork refers specifically to wood milled for use in buildings. Often the terms *millwork* and *moldings* are used synonymously to refer to profiled trim.

Miter A joint that forms a corner. Usually both sides are chopped at a 45-degree angle to form a 90-degree corner.

Moisture content The amount of water contained in a piece of wood; usually expressed as a percentage of the weight of wood that has been dried in an oven to remove all the water.

Mortise A square or rectangular hole cut in wood to receive a tenon (a matching wood insert).

Museum rail A rail made by ripping a board at an angle. One side is fastened to a cabinet or bookshelf unit and the other is fastened to the wall, so the angled edges interlock and hold the cabinet or bookshelf securely. This method is often used to hold heavy artwork to walls in museums.

N

Nailer (pneumatic) An air-powered tool used to drive nails.

Nail set A metal punch used to set nails.

Nominal size The size by which a piece of lumber is sold, but which may not reflect its actual, or *dimen-*

sional, size. Example: A 1x4 measures ¾ in. by 3½ in.

O

Ogee A double curve that describes the molding shape commonly used in crown molding and base cap.

Open grain A designation common among painters and finishers for describing woods, such as oak, ash, and chestnut, with large pores in the grain structure.

P

Particleboard Panel stock made from small particles of wood that are mixed with an adhesive and bonded with heat and pressure.

Picture framing (window trim) A way to trim a window with four miters, one in each corner, like the frame around a picture.

Pinch sticks Two sticks held parallel to each other. By sliding them—one in one direction and one in the other—it's possible to measure a space enclosed by two walls.

Plan view A drawing of a building, room, or cabinet that shows the view from above; it is used to establish the layout of architectural elements.

Plinth The base of a pilaster or column. A plinth block is used as the base of the vertical side *casing* on doors to mimic the base of a column.

Plumb Perpendicular to a level line.

Ply A single sheet of veneer in the core of plywood.

Plywood Panel stock made from cross-laminating several layers, or plies, of *veneer.* Often the core veneers are thicker than the finer, higher-grade face *veneer.*

Pocket Typically refers to a recessed cavity built to hold a sliding door in a wall or cabinet.

Pocket screw A method of attaching wood pieces together by boring deep pocket holes from one side, running almost parallel to the face so they penetrate the

end and can't be seen from the opposite face.

Preacher block A jig used to find the angle of a piece of baseboard that meets a plinth block or door casing.

Q

Quarter measure Rough lumber size denoting thickness in quarters of an inch. 4/4 lumber is four-quarters or 1 in. thick; 5/4 is five-quarters or 1¼ in. thick, and so on. When dressed, the lumber thickness is less. For example, 4/4 lumber dresses out to ¾ in., 5/4 dresses out to 1 in. (or sometimes 1⅛ in.), and so on.

R

Ray fleck In quartersawn wood, this is the figure made when a ray is cut. Rays are strips of cells extending radially within a tree that serve primarily to store food and transport it horizontally in the tree. In many woods, the rays are only a few cells thick and not always visible, but they are most prominent in quarter-sawn oak.

Reveal An offset where two pieces of wood come together. A reveal is commonly used between the *casing* and *jamb* for window or door trim. The offset helps mask slight indiscrepancies in the squareness of the window and door unit.

S

S3S "Surfaced three sides." This denotes hardwood lumber that has been planed on the two faces with one edge ripped straight and the second edge left rough.

S4S "Surfaced four sides." This denotes hardwood lumber that has been planed on both faces and both edges.

Sanitary base A small, milled baseboard stock; the equivalent of *clamshell* for baseboard.

Sapwood The lighter grain in a board that is cut from the outer portion of a tree. When the tree was cut, the sapwood was the living

cells in the trunk that carried sap to the upper portions of the tree. Compare *heartwood.*

Scarf joint A splice made by overlapping two angled cuts in a piece of trim. The angle may be cut as a *bevel* or along the face of the board or both.

Scotia A concave molding commonly used for horizontal transitions.

Scribing A method for transferring an irregular or contoured shape along the edge of a board. This line can then be cut so the board fits tight against the irregular or contoured shape.

Section view A drawing that shows the relationship of parts in an assembly. It depicts what the assembly would look like if a slice had been taken through the assembly.

Shake A defect in wood that occurs when the grain separates along the annual growth rings.

Sheet goods (panel stock) Any type of laminated or pressed lumber sold in sheets. The standard size for one sheet is 4 ft. by 8 ft.

Shelf standard A shelf support that is typically recessed into a groove in the sides of the shelf.

Shim Any thin piece of wood used as a spacer. Typically refers to the thin, tapered pieces of cedar that are used to level a cabinet or to fill the gap between a window or door *jamb* and the rough opening.

Shoe molding A small molding used to cover the gap between the bottom edge of baseboard and the floor. Shoe molding is typically rounded and is a bit taller than it is wide.

Shoot board A jig made to guide a circular saw along a straight line; typically used for crosscutting panel stock or undercutting a door.

Short point The heel of a miter.

Sill The horizontal base of a window. The sill runs perpendicular to the *casing,* much like a jamb, but it typically projects into the room, past the face of the casing. An interior windowsill is often referred to as a *stool* to distinguish it from the exterior sill, which is pitched to allow water to drain off it.

Slip-matched veneer *Veneer* made from a sheet in a *flitch* that is slid across the sheet beneath and spliced at the joints without turning it.

Span The distance between two bearing points.

Splint A stiffener that spans a joint and helps hold it together.

Spring angle The angle between the wall and a *crown* molding. Crown molding is often defined in relation to its spring angle, because that determines the bevel on the back face of the crown molding.

Stickers Thin pieces of wood inserted between the boards that allow air to circulate and help the wood acclimate to indoor humidity levels.

Stool A term used for the level interior windowsill to distinguish it from the pitched or sloped sill on the exterior.

Story pole A stick used to transfer the height of architectural elements around a room. A story pole is typically held vertically and marked with the elevations of the baseboard, windowsill, countertops, chair rail, picture rail, and so on.

Stringer The diagonal framing member in a stair carriage that supports the treads.

Stud The vertical framing members in a wood-framed wall.

Surform A hand tool that resembles a cheese grater and is used to shave the edges of drywall.

T

Takeoff A list of dimensions, or estimated prices, for all the materials needed to complete a project.

Tearout The splintered edges of a cut.

T&G Tongue-and-groove boards have a groove along one edge and a tongue along the other. When installed, the tongue of one board mates with the groove on the adjacent board. Typically, T&G is nailed only on the tongue side, allowing the boards to expand and contract with climate changes.

Tight grain A designation common with painters and finishers for describing wood grain that has small pores in the grain structure, resulting in a dense, smooth surface.

Twist A deformation of a board that occurs when the edges *warp* in a twist, so part of the face curves one direction and part curves in another direction.

V

Veneer A very thin layer of wood. While veneers can be applied to almost any type of wood substrate, it most often is used to face plywood.

W

Wainscoting The decorative panels that cover the bottom 3 ft. to 4 ft. of a wall. Wainscoting typically sits on the baseboard and is capped by a *chair rail*.

Wane The edge of a board that is covered by bark or the outermost edge of the log from which the board was cut. *Waney* is used to describe the edges of a board.

Warp Any distortion in a board that bends it out of its proper flat shape with square edges.

INDEX